P9-DHA-060

Country Ribbon Crafts

Country Ribbon Crafts

Delightful Projects Using Easy Techniques

Cookie Lyday

A STERLING/CHAPELLE BOOK
Sterling Publishing Co., Inc. New York

For Chapelle Ltd.
Owner: *Jo Packham*

Staff: *Trice Boerens, Malissa Boatwright, Rebecca Christensen, Holly Fuller, Cherie Hanson, Holly Hollingsworth, Susan Jorgensen, Amanda McPeck, Tammy Perkins, Jamie C. Pierce, Leslie Ridenour, Amy Vineyard, Nancy Whitley, and Lorrie Young.*

Photographer: *Ryne Hazen*

The photographs in this book were taken at the home of Jo Packham.

Library of Congress Cataloging-in-Publication Data

Lyday, Cookie.
Country ribbon crafts : delightful projects using easy techniques / by Cookie Lyday.
p. cm.
"A Sterling/Chapelle book."
Includes index.
ISBN 0-8069-0990-0
1. Ribbon work. I. Title.
TT850.5.193 1995 94-35542
746'.0476—dc20 CIP

10 9 8 7 6 5 4 3 2 1

A Sterling/Chapelle Book

Published by Sterling Publishing Company, Inc.
387 Park Avenue South, New York, N.Y. 10016

Distributed in Canada by Sterling Publishing
c/o Canadian Manda Group, One Atlantic Avenue, Suite 105
Toronto, Ontario, Canada M6K 3E7
Distributed in Great Britain and Europe by Cassell PLC
Villiers House, 41/47 Strand, London WC2N 5JE, England
Distributed in Australia by Capricorn Link (Australia) Pty Ltd.
P.O. Box 6651, Baulkham Hills, Business Center, NSW 2153, Australia
Printed and bound in Hong Kong

Sterling ISBN 0-8069-0990-0

About the Author

Cookie Lyday is an accomplished artist specializing in ribbon work. Her given name is Cecelia Ann Lyday, after both her grandmothers. She has a Bachelor of Arts degree from the University of South Carolina. She is a wife of thirty years and mother of two children.

Cookie created Beyond the Garden Gate, a company that wholesales her ribbon crafts. The business began in 1992, when she became intrigued by the possibilities of wired ribbons. She worked with different techniques, but says she was "too lazy" to sew. Then she discovered fabric glue and ever since her work has thrived. She finds her ribbon craft creative, relaxing, fast and easy, portable, inexpensive, and most of all FUN!

Contents

General Instructions

Terms & Techniques

Glue–To glue ribbon, use the smallest amount needed of a good quality, quick-tack fabric glue. Let dry between applications. When gluing onto a pillow, it is suggested that you use pins to hold objects in place until dry. To glue jewelry backs or thick wire, cord or rattail, tacky glue or hot glue and a glue gun is recommended.

Ombre–This refers to the shaded ribbons as one color gradually fades to another.

Ribbon Widths– #2 = $^{1}/_{2}$"
#3 = $^{5}/_{8}$"
#5 = 1"
#9 = 1$^{1}/_{2}$"
#12 = 2"
#22 = 2$^{5}/_{8}$"

Stem Wire–Unless otherwise noted in the instructions, 18-gauge stem wire is used in all projects calling for stem wire.

Stuffing–Projects in this book are stuffed with fiberfill or cotton balls.

Patterns–Use tracing paper to trace patterns. Be sure to transfer all information. All patterns include seam allowances. The seam allowance is $^{1}/_{4}$" unless otherwise specified.

Slipstitch–Insert needle at A, taking a small stitch, and slide it through the folded edge of the fabric about $^{1}/_{8}$" to $^{1}/_{4}$", bringing it out at B; see Diagram A.

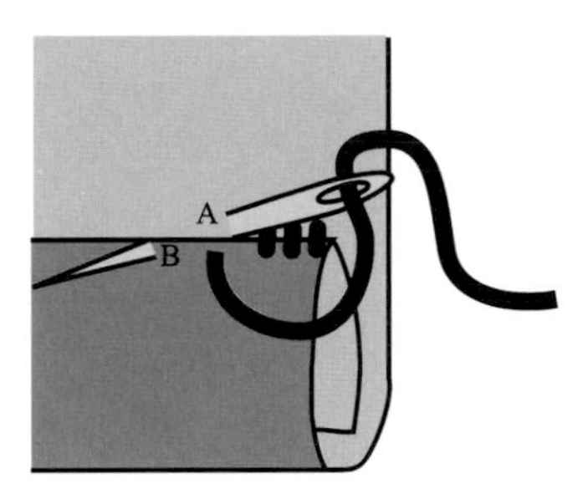

DIAGRAM A

Flowers

Pansies–Each pansy requires 6" of stem wire and $5^3/_4$" of $1^1/_2$" wired ribbon. The ribbon can be ombre, solid, or contrasting.

To make petals, cut two $1^1/_4$" pieces of the same colored ribbon. Glue top raw end of one $1^1/_4$" ribbon length forward $^1/_8$". While glue is still pliable, place a round toothpick at an angle against the corner on the raw folded-edge side of the ribbon; see Diagram B. Roll ribbon around toothpick between thumb and forefinger one or two revolutions. Repeat with other corner. Glue and pinch opposite end, forming a petal; see Diagram B. Repeat with other piece of ribbon. Overlap petals and glue at pinched ends; see Diagram B.

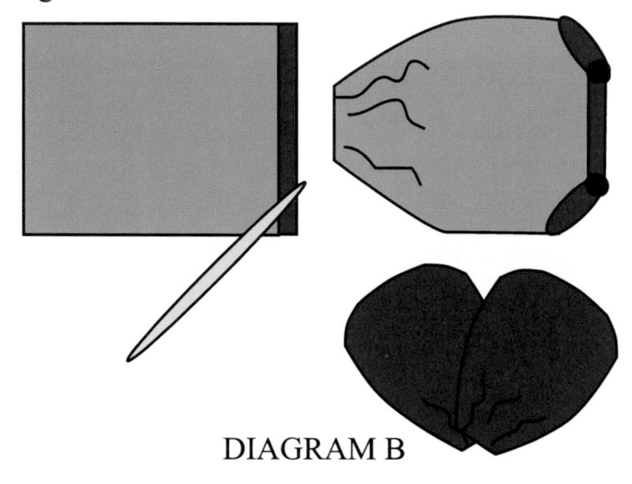

DIAGRAM B

Cut two 1" pieces of the same-colored ribbon. Repeat process above. Glue these petals, overlapping each other, on top of other petals; see Diagram C.

DIAGRAM C

Make a $^1/_2$" elongated hook on one end of the 6" length of stem wire. Place and glue hooked end in center of petals; see Diagram C. (Omit this step when making earrings and pins.)

Cut one $1^1/_4$" piece of ribbon and make a petal. Glue this petal, right sides together, to other petals. Pull this petal forward and down. With fabric pen, make fine lines from center of flower out towards rolled ends of petal.

Violets–Each violet requires 6" of stem wire and 4" of 5/8" ribbon.

To make petals, cut 4" ribbon length into four 1" pieces. Put a bead of glue along one raw end and fold corners in, making a point. Put a dot of glue on point and fold forward, bringing point to edge of folded corners; see Diagram D. Glue and pinch opposite end, making a petal.

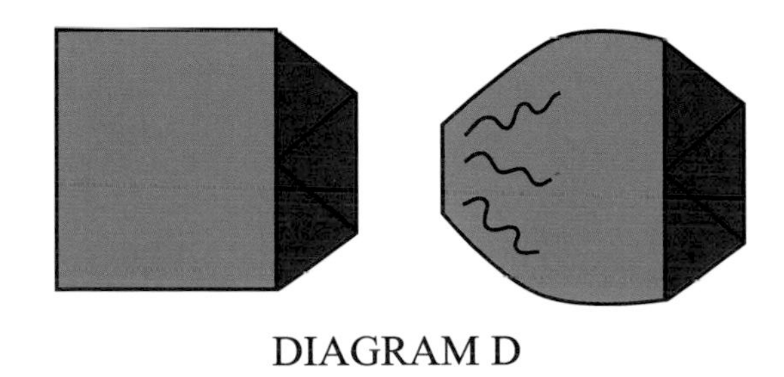

DIAGRAM D

Make a 1/2" elongated hook on one end of the 6" length of stem wire. With right sides in, place and glue pinched end of the four petals around hooked end of wire; see Diagram E. Bend petals open, showing tip of hooked stem wire as stamen. To make a bud, use three petals and glue to wire with right sides out.

DIAGRAM E

<u>Daisies</u>–Each daisy requires 6" of stem wire, 1 1/2" of 1 1/2" wired ribbon, and ribbon for petals in the amount called for in specific instructions.

Make a 1/2" elongated hook on one end of the 6" length of stem wire. Wrap a portion of a cotton ball around the hook. Cover cotton ball with 1 1/2" length of 1 1/2" wired ribbon, making daisy center. Wrap and secure ribbon to wire with thread; see Diagram F. Cut away excess ribbon, being careful not to cut through thread.

DIAGRAM F

To make petals, cut the amount and size of ribbon called for in the specific instructions. On one petal, fold top corners on one raw end of ribbon forward, making a point; glue. Pinch other raw end and glue to underside of daisy center; see Diagram G.

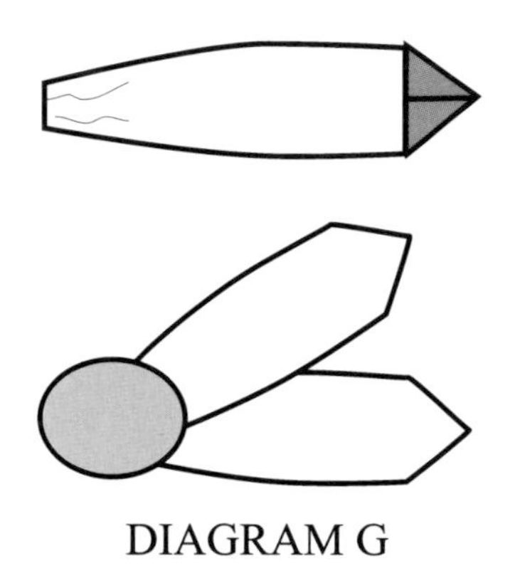

DIAGRAM G

Daffodils–Each daffodil requires 6" of stem wire and $10^1/_2$" of $1^1/_2$" ribbon.

Make a $^1/_2$" elongated hook on one end of the 6" length of stem wire. Cut a 3" length of wired ribbon. Overlap and glue raw ends of ribbon length, forming a tube. Gather and glue one long edge of tube around hooked end of wire, forming a cup; see Diagram H.

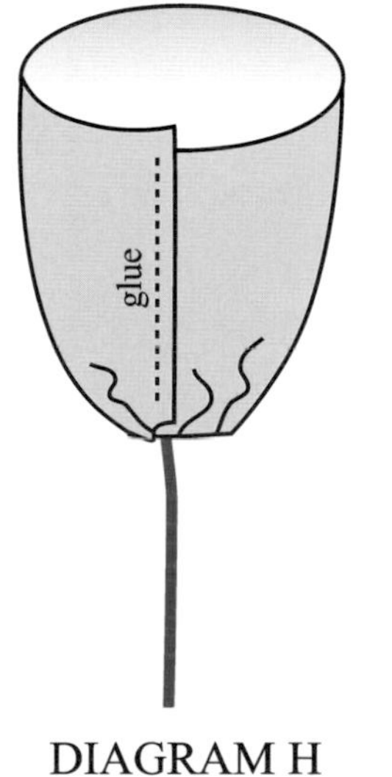

DIAGRAM H

Cut remaining wired ribbon into five $1^1/_2$" lengths. Make five pointed petals; see instructions for "Pointed" leaves on page 16.

Glue petals to gathered end of tube, forming daffodil; see Diagram I.

DIAGRAM I

<u>Rosebuds</u>–Each rosebud requires 6" of stem wire, 2" of 1" ribbon, and a small amount of stuffing.

Make a 1/2" elongated hook around stuffing on one end of the 6" length of stem wire.

To make petals, cut ribbon length into two equal pieces. Glue top raw end of one 1" ribbon length forward 1/8". While glue is still pliable, place a round toothpick at an angle against the corner on the raw folded-edge side of the ribbon; see Diagram J. Roll ribbon around toothpick between thumb and forefinger one or two revolutions. Repeat with other corner. Glue and pinch opposite end, forming a petal; see Diagram J. Repeat with other piece of ribbon. Overlap petals, covering stuffing, and glue to wire at pinched ends; see Diagram J.

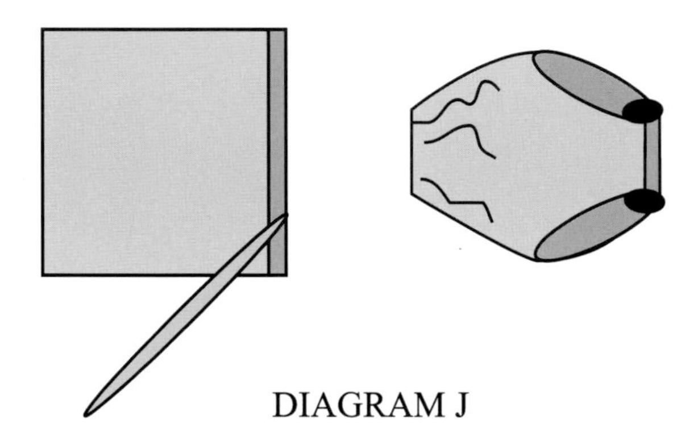

DIAGRAM J

With right sides out, place and glue pinched end of the two petals around hooked end of wire; see Diagram K. To make a mature bud, make three more petals and glue to wire with right sides in.

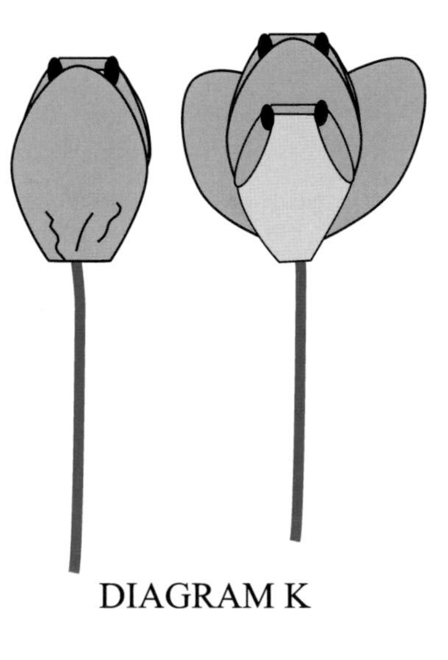

DIAGRAM K

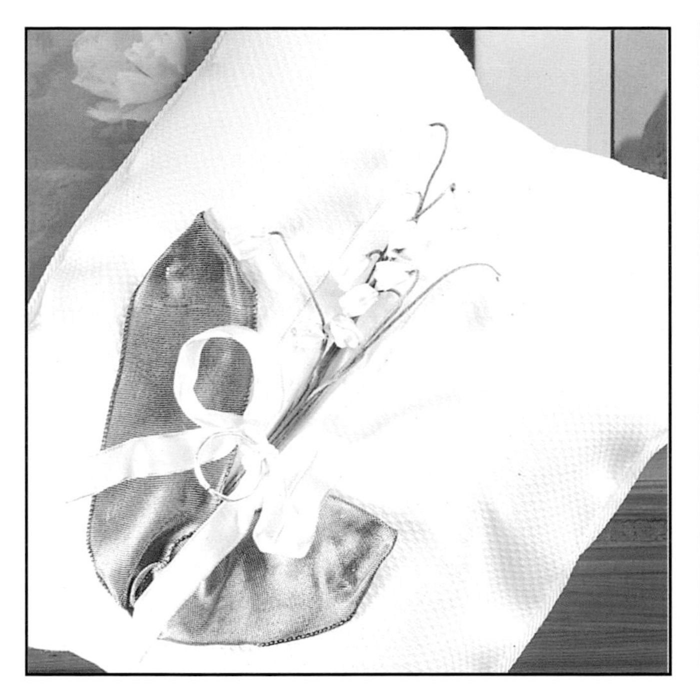

Lilies of the Valley–Each lily of the valley requires 6" of stem wire and 1" of 5/8" ribbon.

Makc a 1/2" elongated hook on one end of the 6" length of stem wire.

Overlap and glue raw short ends of ribbon length, forming a tube. Gather one long edge of tube around hooked end of wire, forming a cup. Gather and glue remaining long edge; see Diagram L.

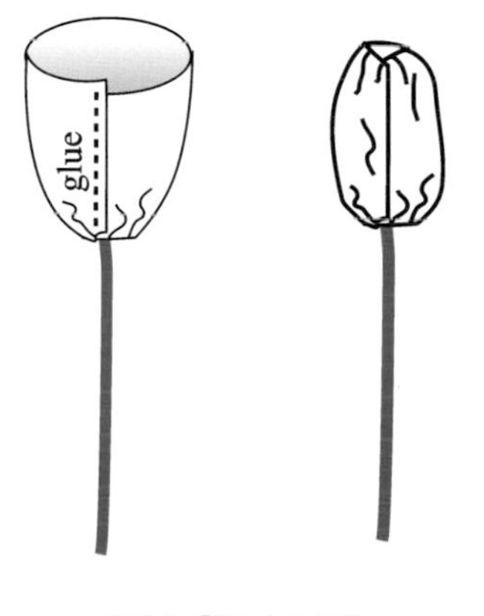

DIAGRAM L

Nasturtiums–Each nasturtium requires 7 1/2" of 1 1/2" ribbon.

To make petals, cut ribbon into five 1 1/2" pieces. Put a bead of glue along one raw end and fold corners in, making a point. Put a dot of glue on point and fold forward, bringing point to edge of folded corners. Glue and pinch opposite end, making a petal; see Diagram M.

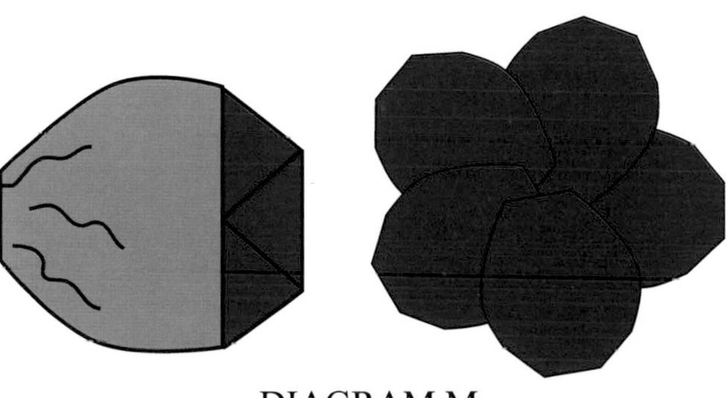

DIAGRAM M

Glue petals together at pinched ends, overlapping. Spread petals, to create a swirling effect; see Diagram M.

Leaves

Heart-Shaped–Cut ribbon into lengths called for in specific instructions. On one raw end, fold and glue corners forward, making a point. Fold opposite end over $^1/_8$" and glue. Put a dot of glue on each folded corner and fold forward slightly, making a blunt point; see Diagram N. Put a drop of glue in the center and on the edge of the blunt point and pinch, making a heart shape; see Diagram N.

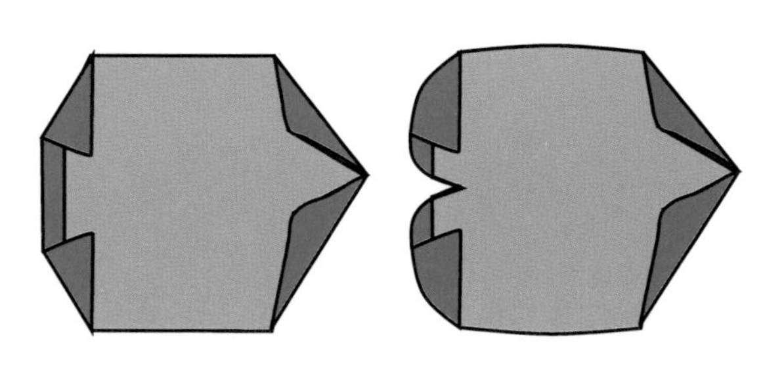

DIAGRAM N

Pointed–Cut ribbon into lengths called for in specific instructions. On one raw end, fold and glue corners forward, making a point. Pinch and glue opposite raw end; see Diagram O.

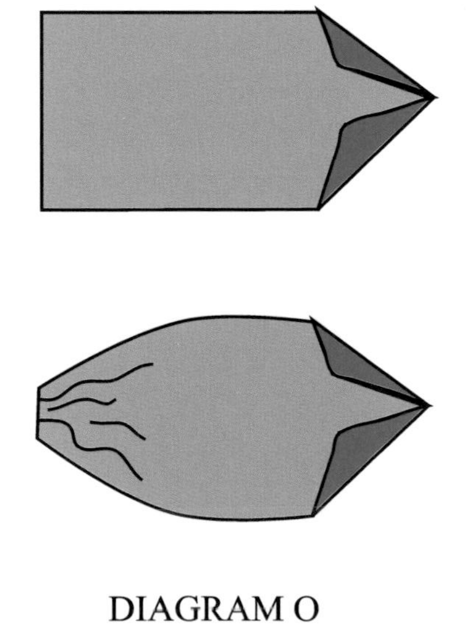

DIAGRAM O

Pansy–Cut ribbon into lengths called for in specific instructions. Fold raw ends forward 1/8"; glue. On one end, fold corners over slightly, making a blunt point; glue. Pinch and glue opposite end; see Diagram P.

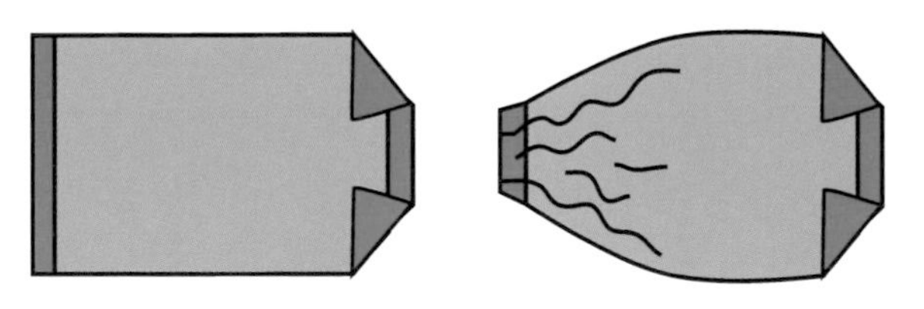

DIAGRAM P

Octagon–cut ribbon into lengths called for in specific instructions. Put a bead of glue along one raw end; fold forward 1/8". Put a drop of glue on folded corners and fold forward slightly, making a blunt point. Repeat with opposite end. On one edge, pinch, forming a V shape; see Diagram Q.

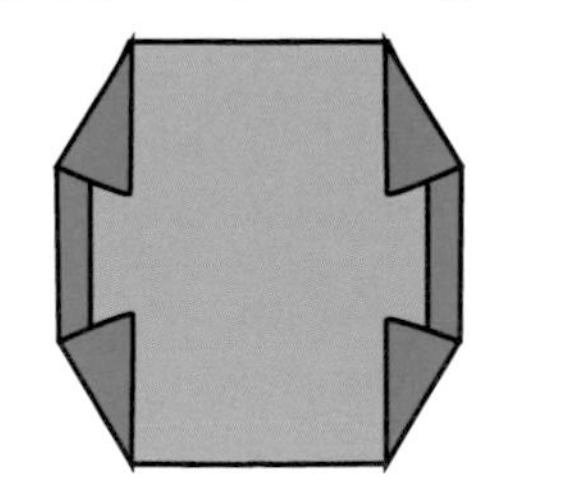

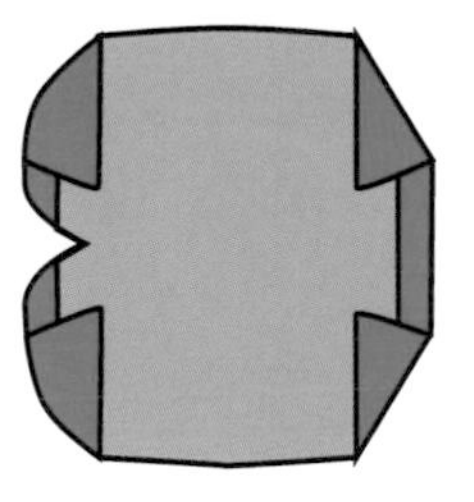

DIAGRAM Q

Leaf Caps–Cut ribbon into lengths called for in specific instructions. Put a thin bead of glue along one raw end; fold forward $^{1}/_{8}$". Repeat on opposite end. Center object to be capped on ribbon length; see Diagram R. (If the object is attached to stem wire, poke a small hole in center of ribbon and slip wire through it.) Fold and glue ribbon over object, making a triangle; see Diagram R. Match opposite corners, making a second triangle and glue; see Diagram R.

Berries–Cut ribbon into lengths called for in specific instructions. Put a thin bead of glue along one raw end and overlap opposite end, making a cone-shaped tube; see Diagram S. With thumbs and forefingers, pleat the thinner end, closing off the open, thin end. Place a drop of glue inside the pleated end and hold until glue bonds. Stuff tube with cotton. Pleat and glue the opposite end as above. Slightly press ends together to shape; see Diagram S.

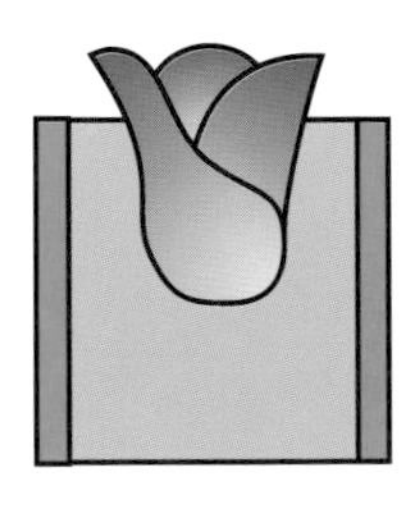

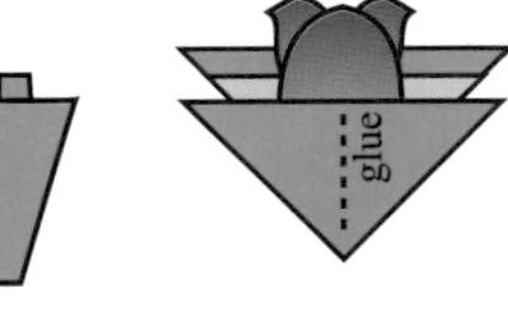

DIAGRAM R

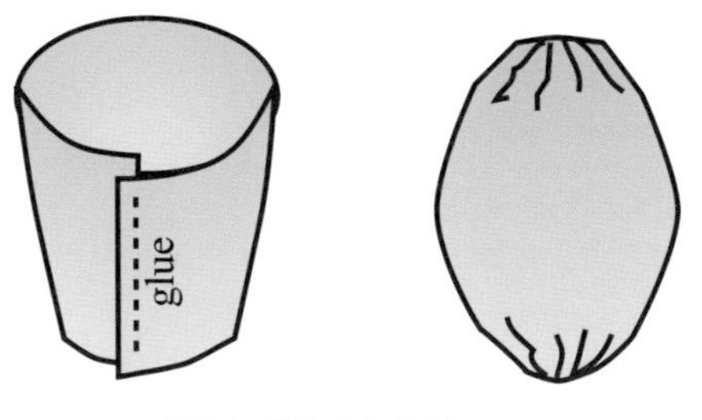

DIAGRAM S

Pots–Cut the brown wired ribbon into two equal lengths. On one length, fold raw short ends over $^{1}/_{4}$" on top edge and $^{1}/_{2}$" on the bottom edge, forming pot; see Diagram T. On remaining ribbon length, fold and glue short raw ends under $^{1}/_{8}$". Fold ribbon length in half lengthwise, and glue to the top wired edge of the pot.

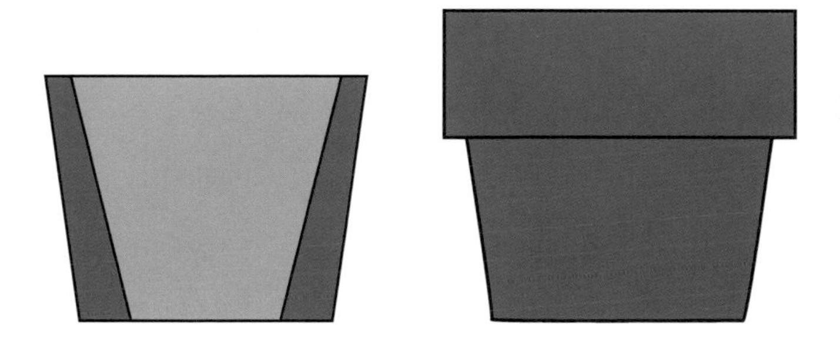

DIAGRAM T

Bees–Each bee requires 1" of $^{1}/_{4}$" cord, 1" of 1" yellow wired ribbon, 1$^{1}/_{2}$" of $^{5}/_{8}$" gold-mesh wired ribbon, and two black artificial stamens.

To make bee, wrap and glue yellow ribbon length around cord. Pinch and glue one end closed. Place stamens in other end and pinch and glue closed. On one raw end of gold-mesh ribbon, fold and glue corners back, forming a point. Fold and glue point back. Repeat on opposite end. Pinch in center and glue to back of bee; see Diagram U.

DIAGRAM U

Chapter One

beyond the garden gate

Pansy Set

Floral Jewelry

Pansy Set

Materials for Bouquet Pin

$^{7}/_{8}$ yard of $1^{1}/_{2}$" wired ribbon in desired colors ($5^{3}/_{4}$" per pansy)
6" of $1^{1}/_{2}$" green wired ribbon
8" of 1" wired ribbon in desired color
$1^{3}/_{8}$ yard of stem wire
One $1^{1}/_{2}$" pinback
Scissors
Quick tack fabric glue
Tacky glue or hot glue gun and glue sticks
Fabric pen

Directions

1. Make five pansies and attach to stem wire; see General Instructions for "Pansies" on page 10.

2. Cut green wired ribbon into three 2" lengths. Make three pansy leaves and attach to stem wire; see General Instructions for "Pansy" leaves on page 17.

3. Using the 8" length of 1" wired ribbon, fold one corner on one raw end so that the raw end is aligned with one long edge of ribbon. Repeat on opposite raw end, creating diagonal finished ends.

4. Bundle the pansies and pansy leaves together. Glue the pinback to the stems at the center of the bundle. Tie the bundle together with the 8" length of ribbon, securing the pinback in place.

Materials for Earrings

$^{3}/_{4}$ yard of $1^{1}/_{2}$" wired ribbon in desired colors ($5^{3}/_{4}$" per pansy)
Four earring backs
Scissors
Quick tack fabric glue
Tacky glue or hot glue gun and glue sticks
Fabric pen

Directions

1. Make four pansies, omitting stem wire; see General Instructions for "Pansies" on page 10.

2. Glue each pansy to one earring back.

Materials for Bar Pin

$^{1}/_{2}$ yard of $1^{1}/_{2}$" wired ribbon in desired colors ($5^{3}/_{4}$" per pansy)
5" of $1^{1}/_{2}$" green wired ribbon
3" x $^{1}/_{2}$" length of heavy plastic
One $1^{1}/_{2}$" pinback
Scissors
Quick tack fabric glue
Tacky glue or hot glue gun and glue sticks
Fabric pen

Directions

1. Make three pansies omitting stem wire; see General Instructions for "Pansies" on page 10.

2. Glue the 5" length of green wired ribbon to length of plastic, wrapping and gluing long edges to back side of plastic. Turn raw fabric ends under $^{1}/_{8}$" and glue.

3. Glue the three pansies to the front side of the ribbon/plastic length.

4. Glue the pinback centered on the back side of the ribbon/plastic length.

Violet Set

Floral Jewelry

Violet Set

Materials for Bouquet Pin

$1^{5}/_{8}$ yards of 1" violet wired ribbon
10" of $1^{1}/_{2}$" green wired ribbon
3 yards of stem wire
One $1^{1}/_{2}$" pinback
Scissors
Quick tack fabric glue
Tacky glue or hot glue gun and glue sticks

Directions

1. Cut violet wired ribbon into fifty-seven 1" lengths. Make twelve violets and three buds; see General Instructions for "Violets" on page 11.

2. Cut green wired ribbon into five 2" lengths. Make five heart-shaped leaves and attach to stem wire; see General Instructions for "Heart-Shaped" leaves on page 16.

3. Bundle the violets, buds, and leaves together. Glue the pinback to the stems at the center of the bundle. Wrap the bundle together with the remaining stem wire, securing the pinback in place.

Materials for Bud Earrings

$^{1}/_{4}$ yard of 1" violet wired ribbon
$3^{1}/_{2}$" of $1^{1}/_{2}$" green wired ribbon
Two earring backs
Scissors
Quick tack fabric glue
Tacky glue or hot glue gun and glue sticks

Directions

1. Cut violet wired ribbon into six 1" lengths. Make three violet buds; see General Instructions for "Violets" on page 11.

2. Cut green wired ribbon into two $1^{3}/_{4}$" lengths. Put a leaf cap on each bud; see General Instructions for "Leaf Caps" on page 18.

3. Glue each violet bud to one earring back.

beyond the garden gate

Floral Jewelry

Daisy Set

Materials for Earrings

$^{3}/_{8}$ yard of $^{5}/_{8}$" white wired ribbon
3" of $1^{1}/_{2}$" yellow wired ribbon
A small amount of stuffing
Two earring backs
Scissors
White sewing thread
Quick tack fabric glue
Tacky glue or hot glue gun and glue sticks

Directions

1. Cut white wired ribbon into twelve 1" lengths. Make twelve daisy petals; see General Instructions for "Daisies" on page 12.

2. Cut yellow wired ribbon into two $1^{1}/_{2}$" lengths. Form two pea-sized balls of stuffing and place one in center of each yellow ribbon length.

3. Gather ribbon around each ball and wrap with thread. Cut away excess ribbon, being careful not to cut through thread.

4. Glue six petals to underside of each daisy center.

5. Glue one daisy to each earring back.

Materials for Pin

$^{3}/_{8}$ yard of $^{5}/_{8}$" white wired ribbon
2" of $1^{1}/_{2}$" yellow wired ribbon
A small amount of stuffing
White sewing thread
One stick pin
Scissors
Quick tack fabric glue
Tacky glue or hot glue gun and glue sticks

Directions

1. Cut white wired ribbon into eight $1^{1}/_{2}$" lengths. Make eight daisy petals; see General Instructions for "Daisies" on page 12.

2. Form a marble-sized ball of stuffing and place in center of yellow ribbon length.

3. Gather ribbon around ball and wrap with thread. Cut away excess ribbon, being careful not to cut through thread.

4. Glue eight petals to underside of daisy center.

5. Glue daisy to stick pin.

Chapter Two

Napkin Rings

Vegetable Set

Napkin Rings

Vegetable Set

Materials for Pea Pods

6" of $1\frac{1}{2}$" ombre white to green wired ribbon
$1\frac{1}{2}$" of $1\frac{1}{2}$" green wired ribbon
$\frac{1}{2}$ yard of 18-gauge stem wire
A small amount of stuffing
Empty paper towel roll
Scissors
Needle-nosed pliers
Quick tack fabric glue
Tacky glue or hot glue gun and glue sticks

Directions

1. To make ring, cut the stem wire in half. Twist the two pieces together with pliers. Wrap twisted wire around paper towel roll, forming a ring. Twist two opposite ends together to secure. Curl the other two into tight coils forming tendrils.

2. Cut ombre wired ribbon into two 3" lengths. Place a small amount of glue on one raw end of one ribbon length and fold corners, forming a point. Repeat at other end. Fold length lengthwise and stuff firmly. Glue long outside edges closed. Pinch ends to shape. Repeat with remaining ribbon length.

3. From green wired ribbon, make a leaf cap, securing pea pods and twisted ends of wire on ring; see General Instructions for "Leaf Caps" on page 18.

Materials for Carrot

12" of 1" ombre green to orange wired ribbon
3" of $\frac{5}{8}$" green wired ribbon
$\frac{1}{2}$ yard of 18-gauge stem wire
A small amount of stuffing
Empty paper towel roll
Scissors
Needle-nosed pliers
Quick tack fabric glue
Tacky glue or hot glue gun and glue sticks

Directions

1. To make ring, cut the stem wire in half. Twist the two pieces together with pliers. Wrap twisted wire around paper towel roll, forming a ring. Twist two opposite ends together to secure. Curl the other two into tight coils forming tendrils.

2. Form stuffing into a 3" carrot-shaped length. With the green edge aligned with the top of the carrot-shaped stuffing, roll the ombre wired ribbon around the stuffing at an angle; see photo. Tuck in the remaining ribbon end at the bottom and glue.

3. Form a tube with green wired ribbon, overlapping and gluing raw ends. Gather one long edge of the tube and glue, forming a cup. Glue cup to top of carrot.

4. Glue carrot to twisted ends of ring.

COOK

Napkin Rings

Vegetable Set

Materials for Pepper

$2^{3}/_{4}$" of $2^{5}/_{8}$" green wired ribbon
$1^{1}/_{2}$" of $1^{1}/_{2}$" green wired ribbon
$^{1}/_{2}$ yard of 18-gauge stem wire
A small amount of stuffing
Empty paper towel roll
Scissors
Needle-nosed pliers
Quick tack fabric glue
Tacky glue or hot glue gun and glue sticks

Directions

1. To make ring, cut the stem wire in half. Twist the two pieces together with pliers. Wrap twisted wire around paper towel roll, forming a ring. Twist two opposite ends together to secure. Curl the other two into tight coils forming tendrils.

2. Place a bead of glue along one raw end of $2^{5}/_{8}$" green wired ribbon. Overlap and glue other raw end, forming a cone-shaped tube. Pinch and glue the narrow end. Stuff moderately. Pinch open end closed and glue.

3. From $1^{1}/_{2}$" green wired ribbon, make a leaf cap, attaching to wide end of pepper; see General Instructions for "Leaf Caps" on page 18.

4. Glue pepper to twisted ends of ring.

Materials for Tomatoes

7" of $1^{1}/_{2}$" ombre red to orange wired ribbon
2" of $^{5}/_{8}$" green wired ribbon
$^{1}/_{2}$ yard of 18-gauge stem wire
A small amount of stuffing
Empty paper towel roll
Scissors
Needle-nosed pliers
Quick tack fabric glue
Tacky glue or hot glue gun and glue sticks

Directions

1. To make ring, cut the stem wire in half. Twist the two pieces together with pliers. Wrap twisted wire around paper towel roll, forming a ring. Twist two opposite ends together to secure. Curl the other two into tight coils forming tendrils.

2. Cut ombre wired ribbon into two equal lengths. Overlap and glue raw ends of one ribbon length, forming a tube. Gather one long edge of tube, forming a cup; glue. Stuff firmly. Gather and glue remaining long edge, closing tube. Repeat with other ribbon length.

3. Cut two 1" lengths of green wired ribbon. Make two leaf caps, attaching to tops of tomatoes; see General Instructions for "Leaf Caps" on page 18.

4. Glue tomatoes to twisted ends of ring.

nish
ettuce leaves. Peel the mango, cut off
them. Trim the rest of the flesh off the
ly (there will be lots of juice), and mix into
the avocado in half, remove the pit, and scoop
rom the skin in 1 piece with a large spoon. Cut
into fans.
isk together the dressing in a medium bowl. Toss the
lettuce leaves with half the dressing and place them on
lad platter. Arrange the mango slices and fanned avocado
top of the lettuce and evenly distribute the remaining
top. Garnish with a few cilantro leaves, if desired.
On left, Butter Lettuces with Mango and
tter, Tomato Arugula Salad (recipe p. 55);
and Red Leaf Lettuces with Oranges,
nnel (recipe p. 54)

Napkin Rings

Vegetable Set

Materials for Eggplant

4" of 2 5/8" dark purple wired ribbon
1 1/2" of 1 1/2" green wired ribbon
1/2 yard of 18-gauge stem wire
A small amount of stuffing
Empty paper towel roll
Scissors
Needle-nosed pliers
Quick tack fabric glue
Tacky glue or hot glue gun and glue sticks

Directions

1. To make ring, cut the stem wire in half. Twist the two pieces together with pliers. Wrap twisted wire around paper towel roll, forming a ring. Twist two opposite ends together to secure. Curl the other two into tight coils forming tendrils.

2. Place a bead of glue along one raw end of dark purple wired ribbon. Overlap and glue other raw end, forming a cone-shaped tube. Pinch and glue the narrow end. Stuff firmly. Pinch open end closed and glue.

3. From green wired ribbon, make a leaf cap, attaching to wide end of eggplant; see General Instructions for "Leaf Caps" on page 18.

4. Glue eggplant to twisted ends of ring.

Materials for Cabbage

1/2 yard of 1 1/2" ombre green to purple wired ribbon
1/2 yard of 18-gauge stem wire
A small amount of stuffing
Empty paper towel roll
Scissors
Needle-nosed pliers
Quick tack fabric glue
Tacky glue or hot glue gun and glue sticks

Directions

1. To make ring, cut the stem wire in half. Twist the two pieces together with pliers. Wrap twisted wire around paper towel roll, forming a ring. Twist two opposite ends together to secure. Curl the other two into tight coils forming tendrils.

2. Cut a 3 1/2" length of ombre wired ribbon. Overlap and glue raw ends, forming a tube. Gather one long edge of tube, forming a cup; glue. Stuff. Gather and glue remaining long edge, closing tube.

3. Cut the remaining ribbon into four 2" lengths and four 1 1/2" lengths. Fold one raw end over 1/8"; glue. Fold corners in slightly; see photo. Repeat for all ribbon lengths. Pinch and glue raw ends of 1 1/2" lengths right side out (2" lengths right side in) to green end of cabbage.

4. Glue cabbage to twisted ends of ring.

Fruit Set

to pin to
oneself
as a rose
jewel
but doubtless God never did
a carpet of wild strawberries
where berries lie
in hidden clusters
Strawberries: eaten at all mens tables in the summer,

Napkin Rings

Fruit Set

Materials for Peach

12" of $1\frac{1}{2}$" ombre rose to peach wired ribbon
$1\frac{1}{2}$" of $1\frac{1}{2}$" green wired ribbon
$\frac{1}{2}$ yard of 18-gauge stem wire
A small amount of stuffing
Empty paper towel roll
Scissors
Needle-nosed pliers
Quick tack fabric glue
Tacky glue or hot glue gun and glue sticks

Directions

1. To make ring, cut the stem wire in half. Twist the two pieces together with pliers. Wrap twisted wire around paper towel roll, forming a ring. Twist two opposite ends together to secure. Curl the other two into tight coils forming tendrils.

2. Cut ombre wired ribbon into two equal lengths. Overlap and glue rose edges of lengths, making a 6" x 3" piece. Overlap and glue raw ends of 6" x 3" piece, forming a tube. Gather one long edge of tube, forming a cup; glue. Stuff lightly. Gather and glue remaining long edge, closing tube.

3. From green wired ribbon, make a pointed leaf, attaching to top of peach; see General Instructions for "Pointed" leaves on page 16.

4. Glue peach to twisted ends of ring.

Materials for Plum

4" of $2\frac{5}{8}$" dark purple wired ribbon
$\frac{1}{2}$" of brown rattail
$\frac{1}{2}$ yard of 18-gauge stem wire
A small amount of stuffing
Empty paper towel roll
Scissors
Needle-nosed pliers
Quick tack fabric glue
Tacky glue or hot glue gun and glue sticks

Directions

1. To make ring, cut the stem wire in half. Twist the two pieces together with pliers. Wrap twisted wire around paper towel roll, forming a ring. Twist two opposite ends together to secure. Curl the other two into tight coils forming tendrils.

2. Place a bead of glue along one raw end of dark purple wired ribbon. Overlap and glue other raw end, forming a cone-shaped tube. Pinch and glue the narrow end. Stuff firmly. Pinch open end around piece of rattail for stem. Glue end closed, securing stem.

3. Glue plum to twisted ends of ring.

Fruit Set

Napkin Rings

Fruit Set

Materials for Strawberries

6" of 1 1/2" ombre red to pink wired ribbon
3" of 1 1/2" green wired ribbon
1/2 yard of 18-gauge stem wire
A small amount of stuffing
Empty paper towel roll
Scissors
Needle-nosed pliers
Quick tack fabric glue
Tacky glue or hot glue gun and glue sticks

Directions

1. To make ring, cut the stem wire in half. Twist the two pieces together with pliers. Wrap twisted wire around paper towel roll, forming a ring. Twist two opposite ends together to secure. Curl the other two into tight coils forming tendrils.

2. Cut ombre wired ribbon into two 3" lengths. Make two berries; see General Instructions for "Berries" on page 18.

3. Cut green wired ribbon into two equal lengths. Make two leaf caps, attaching one to each strawberry top; see General Instructions for "Leaf Caps" on page 18.

4. Glue strawberries to twisted ends of ring.

Materials for Cherries

7" of 1 1/2" dark red wired ribbon
1" of brown rattail
1/2 yard of 18-gauge stem wire
A small amount of stuffing
Empty paper towel roll
Scissors
Needle-nosed pliers
Quick tack fabric glue
Tacky glue or hot glue gun and glue sticks

Directions

1. To make ring, cut the stem wire in half. Twist the two pieces together with pliers. Wrap twisted wire around paper towel roll, forming a ring. Twist two opposite ends together to secure. Curl the other two into tight coils forming tendrils.

2. Cut red wired ribbon into two equal lengths. Overlap and glue raw ends of one ribbon length, forming a tube. Gather one long edge of tube, forming a cup; glue. Stuff firmly. Gather remaining open edge around piece of rattail for stem. Glue edge closed, securing stem. Repeat with other ribbon length.

3. Glue cherries to twisted ends of ring.

PER&TEA

Napkin Rings

Fruit Set

Materials for Blackberries

5" of $1^1/_2$" black wired ribbon
Red fabric paint
Paintbrush
$^1/_2$ yard of 18-gauge stem wire
A small amount of stuffing
Empty paper towel roll
Scissors
Needle-nosed pliers
Quick tack fabric glue
Tacky glue or hot glue gun and glue sticks

Directions

1. To make ring, cut the stem wire in half. Twist the two pieces together with pliers. Wrap twisted wire around paper towel roll, forming a ring. Twist two opposite ends together to secure. Curl the other two into tight coils forming tendrils.

2. Cut black wired ribbon into two equal lengths. Paint small red dots on ribbon; let dry. Make two berries; see General Instructions for "Berries" on page 18.

3. Glue blackberries to twisted ends of ring.

Materials for Apple

12" of $1^1/_2$" ombre red to pink wired ribbon
$1^1/_2$" of 1" green wired ribbon
$^1/_2$ yard of 18-gauge stem wire
A small amount of stuffing
Empty paper towel roll
Scissors
Needle-nosed pliers
Quick tack fabric glue
Tacky glue or hot glue gun and glue sticks

Directions

1. To make ring, cut the stem wire in half. Twist the two pieces together with pliers. Wrap twisted wire around paper towel roll, forming a ring. Twist two opposite ends together to secure. Curl the other two into tight coils forming tendrils.

2. Cut ombre wired ribbon into two equal lengths. Overlap and glue red edges of lengths, making a 6" x 3" piece. Overlap and glue raw ends of 6" x 3" piece, forming a tube. Gather one long edge of tube, forming a cup; glue. Stuff lightly. Gather and glue remaining long edge, closing tube.

3. Make a pointed leaf, attaching to top of apple; see General Instructions for "Pointed" leaves on page 16.

4. Glue apple to twisted ends of ring.

Napkin Rings

Assorted Set

Materials for Holly

6" of $1^1/_2$" metallic-gold-mesh wired ribbon
4" of $1^1/_2$" dark green wired ribbon
3" of $1^1/_2$" red wired ribbon
A small amount of stuffing
Red sewing thread
Scissors
Quick tack fabric glue
Tacky glue or hot glue gun and glue sticks

Directions

1. To make ring, overlap and glue raw ends of $1^1/_2$" metallic-gold ribbon, forming a tube. Pinch edges together at seam and glue.

2. Cut dark green wired ribbon into two equal lengths. Make two pointed leaves; see General Instructions for "Pointed" leaves on page 16.

3. Cut red wired ribbon into three 1" lengths. Form three pea-sized balls of stuffing and place one in center of each red ribbon length.

4. Gather ribbon around each ball and wrap with thread, making three holly berries. Cut away excess ribbon, being careful not to cut through thread.

5. Glue two leaves and three holly berries to pinched seam of ring.

Materials for Bird Nest

6" of $1^1/_2$" metallic-gold-mesh wired ribbon
1" of 1" green wired ribbon
A small amount of gold floral hair
One small twig
Metallic-gold paint
Paintbrush
A small amount of stuffing
Scissors
Quick tack fabric glue
Tacky glue or hot glue gun and glue sticks

Directions

1. To make ring, overlap and glue raw ends of $1^1/_2$" metallic-gold ribbon, forming a tube. Pinch edges together at seam and glue.

2. Make a pointed leaf from green wired ribbon; see General Instructions for "Pointed" leaves on page 16.

3. Paint twig gold; let dry.

4. Form floral hair into a small nest.

5. Glue twig and leaf to pinched seam of ring. Glue nest on top.

Floral Set

"Light gives me the beauty",
said the flower. "Yes, but air
gives you life", whispered the
poet's voice!"

Napkin Rings

Floral Set

Materials for Daffodil

10 1/2" of 1 1/2" yellow wired ribbon
1/2 yard of 18-gauge stem wire
Empty paper towel roll
Scissors
Needle-nosed pliers
Quick tack fabric glue
Tacky glue or hot glue gun and glue sticks

Directions

1. To make ring, cut the stem wire in half. Twist the two pieces together with pliers. Wrap twisted wire around paper towel roll, forming a ring. Twist two opposite ends together to secure. Curl the other two into tight coils forming tendrils.

2. Make a daffodil and attach to stem wire; see General Instructions for "Daffodils" on page 13.

3. Glue daffodil to twisted ends of ring.

Materials for Morning Glory

11" of 1 1/2" ombre blue to white wired ribbon
3" of 1 1/2" green wired ribbon
1/2 yard of 18-gauge stem wire
Empty paper towel roll
Scissors
Needle-nosed pliers
Quick tack fabric glue
Tacky glue or hot glue gun and glue sticks

Directions

1. To make ring, cut the stem wire in half. Twist the two pieces together with pliers. Wrap twisted wire around paper towel roll, forming a ring. Twist two opposite ends together to secure. Curl the other two into tight coils forming tendrils.

2. Cut a 3" length from ombre wired ribbon. Overlap and glue raw ends of ribbon length, forming a tube. Gather white long edge of tube, forming a cup; glue. Repeat with remaining ombre ribbon, except gather and glue to fit blue edge of smaller tube.

3. Cut green wired ribbon in half. Make one leaf cap, and one heart-shaped leaf; see General Instructions for "Leaf Caps" and "Heart-Shaped" leaves on pages 18 and 16 respectively.

4. Glue leaf to twisted ends of ring. Glue morning glory on top.

Floral Set

Napkin Rings

Floral Set

Materials for Daisy

$^3/_8$ yard of $^5/_8$" white wired ribbon
$1^1/_2$" of $1^1/_2$" yellow wired ribbon
$1^1/_2$" of $1^1/_2$" green wired ribbon
$^1/_2$ yard of 18-gauge stem wire
A small amount of stuffing
Empty paper towel roll
Scissors
Needle-nosed pliers
Quick tack fabric glue
Tacky glue or hot glue gun and glue sticks

Directions

1. To make ring, cut the stem wire in half. Twist the two pieces together with pliers. Wrap twisted wire around paper towel roll, forming a ring. Twist two opposite ends together to secure. Curl the other two into tight coils forming tendrils.

2. Cut white wired ribbon into eight $1^1/_2$" lengths. Make an eight-petaled daisy, omitting stem wire; see General Instructions for "Daisies" on page 12.

3. From green wired ribbon, make a pointed leaf, attaching to underside of daisy; see General Instructions for "Pointed" leaves on page 16.

4. Glue daisy to twisted ends of ring.

Materials for Pansy

$5^3/_4$ yard of $1^1/_2$ " rose wired ribbon
$1^1/_2$ " of $1^1/_2$ " green wired ribbon
$^1/_2$ yard of 18-gauge stem wire
Empty paper towel roll
Black fabric pen
Scissors
Needle-nosed pliers
Quick tack fabric glue
Tacky glue or hot glue gun and glue sticks

Directions

1. To make ring, cut the stem wire in half. Twist the two pieces together with pliers. Wrap twisted wire around paper towel roll, forming a ring. Twist two opposite ends together to secure. Curl the other two into tight coils forming tendrils.

2. Make a pansy from rose wired ribbon; see General Instructions for "Pansies" on page 10.

3. From green wired ribbon, make a pansy leaf, attaching to underside of pansy; see General Instructions for "Pansy" leaves on page 17.

4. Glue pansy to twisted ends of ring.

Chapter Three

Wedding Accessories

Daisy Set

Wedding Accessories

Daisy Set

Materials for Ring Pillow

1/4 yard of white organdy fabric
1/4 yard of white and yellow gingham fabric
White sewing thread
1 yard of 5/8" white wired ribbon
4 1/2" of 1 1/2" yellow wired ribbon
4 1/2" of 1 1/2" green wired ribbon
24" of 1/4" white silk ribbon
24" of 1/4" green silk ribbon
1 yard of 18-gauge stem wire
Stuffing
Scissors
Quick tack fabric glue
Tacky glue or hot glue gun and glue sticks

Directions

1. Cut a 10" x 27" piece of white organdy fabric. Fold short ends over 1/4" to wrong side; press. With right sides facing and short ends overlapping 2 1/2", sew a 1/4" seam along long raw edges. Turn and press. Topstitch 1 1/2" all around from outside edges, forming a pocket for pillow.

2. Cut two 7" x 9" pieces of white and yellow gingham fabric. With right sides facing, sew a 1/4" seam along all edges, leaving a small opening for turning. Turn and stuff lightly. Slipstitch opening closed. Insert pillow in pocket of organdy.

3. Cut twenty-four 1 1/2" lengths from white wired ribbon and three 1 1/2" lengths from yellow wired ribbon. Make three eight-petaled daisies; see General Instructions for "Daisies" on page 12.

4. Cut green wired ribbon into three 1 1/2" lengths. Make three pointed leaves, attaching each to a 6" length of stem wire; see General Instructions for "Pointed" leaves on page 16.

5. Cut four 12" lengths from white and green silk ribbons. Handling all as one, tie a bow around daisy and leaf bouquet. Glue bouquet to center of pillow.

Materials for Bookmark

$^1/_4$ yard of $1^1/_2$" white-mesh wired ribbon
4" of $^5/_8$" white wired ribbon
1" of 1" yellow wired ribbon
$1^1/_2$" of $1^1/_2$" ombre green to white wired ribbon
6" of 18-gauge stem wire
Scissors
Quick tack fabric glue
Tacky glue or hot glue gun and glue sticks

Directions

1. Fold and glue one short end of white-mesh wired ribbon $^1/_8$". Fold again $1^1/_2$"; pinch and glue together. On opposite end, cut 1" up from center. Fold and glue inside edges to long wired edges, making a V-shape; see photo.

2. Cut stem wire into two equal lengths. Cut four 1" lengths from $^5/_8$" white wired ribbon. Make a four-petaled daisy; see General Instructions for "Daisies" on page 12.

3. Make a heart-shaped leaf from ombre wired ribbon; see General Instructions for "Heart-Shaped" leaves on page 16.

4. Glue daisy and leaf to pinched area of bookmark, wrapping stems around bookmark. Curl the ends of the stems into tight coils forming tendrils.

Materials for Shoe Clips

1 yard of $1^1/_2$" white-mesh wired ribbon
16" of $^5/_8$" white wired ribbon
3" of $1^1/_2$" yellow wired ribbon
3" of $1^1/_2$" green wired ribbon
One pair of shoe clip findings
Scissors
Quick tack fabric glue
Tacky glue or hot glue gun and glue sticks

Directions

1. Cut white-mesh wired ribbon into two equal lengths. Tie each length into a bow. Fold and glue inside corner on each end back, creating diagonal finished ends. Glue one bow to each shoe clip finding.

2. Cut twelve $1^1/_2$" lengths from $^5/_8$" white wired ribbon. Make two six-petaled daisies, omitting stem wire; see General Instructions for "Daisies" on page 12.

3. Cut green wired ribbon into two equal lengths. Make two pointed leaves; see General Instructions for "Pointed" leaves on page 16.

4. Glue one daisy and one leaf to center of each bow.

Materials for White Organdy Garter

$^{1}/_{4}$ yard of white organdy fabric
$^{3}/_{8}$ yard of $^{1}/_{4}$" elastic
White sewing thread
24" of $^{5}/_{8}$" white wired ribbon
3" of $1^{1}/_{2}$" yellow wired ribbon
$1^{1}/_{2}$" of $1^{1}/_{2}$" green wired ribbon
$^{1}/_{4}$ yard of 18-gauge stem wire
Scissors
Quick tack fabric glue
Tacky glue or hot glue gun and glue sticks

Directions

1. Cut a $3^{3}/_{4}$" x 45" piece of white organdy fabric. On wrong side of fabric, run a thin bead of glue along long raw edges and roll.

2. Cut a $^{3}/_{4}$" x 45" piece of white organdy fabric. Fold long raw edges under $^{1}/_{4}$"; press. Place on wrong side of $3^{3}/_{4}$" x 45" piece of white organdy fabric, $1^{1}/_{2}$" from one long edge. Sew along top and bottom folded edges, making a casing for elastic.

3. With wrong sides facing, stitch short ends together, leaving casing open.

4. Feed elastic through casing. Stitch ends together.

5. Cut sixteen $1^{1}/_{2}$" lengths from white wired ribbon, two $1^{1}/_{2}$" lengths from yellow wired ribbon, and two 3" lengths of stem wire. Make two eight-petaled daisies; see General Instructions for "Daisies" on page 12.

6. Make a pointed leaf from green wired ribbon, attaching it to remaining 3" length of stem wire; see General Instructions for "Pointed" leaves on page 16.

7. Glue daisies and leaf to garter covering seam.

Materials for White & Yellow Garter

$^{3}/_{4}$ yard of 1$^{1}/_{2}$" yellow wired ribbon
$^{3}/_{4}$ yard of 1" white scalloped trim
$^{3}/_{4}$ yard of $^{1}/_{2}$" white satin ribbon
$^{3}/_{8}$ yard of $^{1}/_{4}$" elastic
White sewing thread
10$^{1}/_{2}$" of $^{5}/_{8}$" white wired ribbon
3" of 1$^{1}/_{2}$" green wired ribbon
Scissors
Quick tack fabric glue
Tacky glue or hot glue gun and glue sticks

Directions

1. Cut one 1$^{1}/_{2}$" length of yellow wired ribbon; set aside. Remove wire from one long edge of remaining yellow ribbon. Overlap the wireless edge of the yellow wired ribbon and the white scalloped trim with the trim on top; topstitch.

2. Place $^{1}/_{2}$" white satin ribbon on wrong side of yellow wired ribbon, 1$^{1}/_{2}$" from long wired edge. Sew along top and bottom edges, making a casing for elastic.

3. With wrong sides facing, stitch short ends together, leaving casing open.

4. Feed elastic through casing. Stitch ends together.

5. Cut seven 1$^{1}/_{2}$" lengths from white wired ribbon. Make a seven-petaled daisy, omitting stem wire; see General Instructions for "Daisies" on page 12.

6. Cut green wired ribbon into two equal lengths. Make two pointed leaves; see General Instructions for "Pointed" leaves on page 16.

7. Glue daisy and leaves to garter covering seam.

Rosebud Set

Wedding Accessories

Rosebud Set

Materials for Ring Pillow

3/8 yard of white cotton pique fabric
White sewing thread
1 yard of white decorative cording
1 yard of 1" pink textured wired ribbon
3/8 yard of 5/8" white wired ribbon
1 1/2" of 1 1/2" yellow wired ribbon
1/2 yard of 1" white wired ribbon
7" of 1" ombre pink to white wired ribbon
3" of 1 1/2" ombre green to white wired ribbon
24" of 1/4" white silk ribbon
2 yards of 18-gauge stem wire
Stuffing
Scissors
Quick tack fabric glue
Tacky glue or hot glue gun and glue sticks

Directions

1. Cut two 8" x 10" pieces of white pique fabric. Baste piping to wrong side of one piece. With right sides facing, sew a 1/4" seam along all edges, sandwiching piping in seam and leaving a small opening for turning. Turn and stuff lightly. Slipstitch opening closed.

2. Cut one 20" length of textured wired ribbon. Wrap and glue around length of pillow with seam at center front. Make a bow with remaining textured ribbon. Fold and glue inside raw corners back, making diagonal finished ends. Glue bow to pillow covering seam.

3. Cut seven 1 1/2" lengths from 5/8" white wired ribbon. Make a seven-petaled daisy; see General Instructions for "Daisies" on page 12.

4. Cut three 1" lengths of 5/8" white wired ribbon. Make three lilies of the valley; see General Instructions for "Lilies of the Valley" on page 15.

5. Cut two 3" lengths and ten 1" lengths from 1" white wired ribbon. Make two daffodils; see General Instructions for "Daffodils" on page 13.

6. From remaining 1" ribbon, make two pansies and attach to stem wire; see General Instructions for "Pansies" on page 10.

7. Make two rosebuds from pink ombre wired ribbon; see general instruction for "Rosebuds" on page 14.

8. Cut ombre green wired ribbon into two 1 1/2" lengths. Make two heart-shaped leaves, attaching each to a 6" length of stem wire; see General Instructions for "Heart-Shaped" leaves on page 16.

9. Cut white silk ribbon into two equal lengths. Handling both as one, tie a bow around bouquet. Glue bouquet to bow on center of pillow.

Materials for White & Pink Garter

3/4 yard of 1 1/2" white-mesh wired ribbon
3/4 yard of 1" pink textured wired ribbon
3/4 yard of 1/2" white satin ribbon
3/8 yard of 1/4" elastic
White sewing thread
5" of 1" ombre pink to white wired ribbon
3" of 1" green wired ribbon
3" of 18-gauge stem wire
Scissors
Quick tack fabric glue
Tacky glue or hot glue gun and glue sticks

Directions

1. Remove wire from one long edge of textured and mesh wired ribbon. Overlap the wireless edges with the textured ribbon on top; topstitch.

2. Place 1/2" white satin ribbon on wrong side of mesh wired ribbon, 1 1/2" from long wired edge. Sew along top and bottom edges, making a casing for elastic.

3. With wrong sides facing, stitch short ends together, leaving casing open.

4. Feed elastic through casing. Stitch ends together.

5. Cut five 1" lengths from ombre wired ribbon. Make a mature rosebud, attaching to stem wire; see General Instructions for "Rosebuds" on page 14.

6. Cut green wired ribbon into two equal lengths. From one length, make a leaf cap; see General Instructions for "Leaf Caps" on page 18. From the remaining length, make a pointed leaf, attaching just below hooked end of stem wire; see General Instructions for "Pointed" leaves on page 16.

7. Glue rosebud to garter covering seam.

Materials for Barrette

1 yard of 1½" white-mesh wired ribbon
1 yard of 1" pink textured wired ribbon
2" of 1" ombre pink to white wired ribbon
10½" of ⅝" white wired ribbon
1½" of 1½" yellow wired ribbon
⅛ yard of 1" green wired ribbon
24" of 18-gauge stem wire
One 3" barrette
Scissors
Quick tack fabric glue
Tacky glue or hot glue gun and glue sticks

Directions

1. From textured and mesh wired ribbon, make two four-looped bows. Fold and glue raw short ends back, making diagonal finished ends. Glue mesh bow and then pink bow to barrette.

2. Cut ⅝" white wired ribbon into seven 1½" lengths. Make a seven-petaled daisy; see General Instructions for "Daisies" on page 12.

3. From ombre wired ribbon, make a rosebud; see General Instructions for "Rosebuds" on page 14.

4. Cut green wired ribbon into three 1½" lengths. Make two pointed leaves and attach to stem wire; see General Instructions for "Pointed" leaves on page 16. From the remaining length of green ribbon, make a leaf cap, covering base of rosebud; see General Instructions for "Leaf Caps" on page 18.

5. Wrap and glue stem wires around center of bows, securing flowers and leaves to barrette.

Materials for Comb

6 1/2" of 1/2" white decorative trim
8" of 5/8" white wired ribbon
1" of 1" yellow wired ribbon
2" of 1" ombre pink to white wired ribbon
5" of 1" white wired ribbon
1/8 yard of 1" green wired ribbon
1 yard of 18-gauge stem wire
One 3" clear plastic comb
Scissors
Quick tack fabric glue
Tacky glue or hot glue gun and glue sticks

Directions

1. Wrap and glue decorative trim around top of comb.

2. Cut 5/8" white wired ribbon into five 1" lengths. Make a five-petaled daisy; see General Instructions for "Daisies" on page 12.

3. Cut remaining 5/8" white wired ribbon into two 1" lengths. Make two lilies of the valley; see General Instructions for "Lilies of the Valley" on page 15.

4. From ombre wired ribbon, make a rosebud; see General Instructions for "Rosebuds" on page 14.

5. Cut green wired ribbon into three 1 1/2" lengths. Make two pointed leaves and attach to stem wire; see General Instructions for "Pointed" leaves on page 16. From the remaining length of green ribbon, make a leaf cap, covering base of rosebud; see General Instructions for "Leaf Caps" on page 18.

6. Wrap and glue stem wires around one end of comb. Curl ends of wire into tight coils, forming tendrils.

Materials for White Garter

3/4 yard of 2 1/2" white wired ribbon
3/4 yard of 1" white satin ribbon
3/8 yard of 1/4" elastic
White sewing thread
2" of 1" ombre pink to white wired ribbon
1 1/2" of 1" green wired ribbon
3" of 18-gauge stem wire
24" of 1/4" green silk ribbon
Scissors
Quick tack fabric glue
Tacky glue or hot glue gun and glue sticks

Directions

1. Place 1" white satin ribbon centered on right side of 2 1/2" white wired ribbon. Topstitch along top and bottom edges, making a casing for elastic.

2. With wrong sides facing, stitch short ends together, leaving casing open.

3. Feed elastic through casing. Stitch ends together.

4. Cut ombre wired ribbon into two equal lengths. Make a rosebud, attaching to stem wire; see General Instructions for "Rosebuds" on page 14.

5. From green wired ribbon, make a pointed leaf, attaching just below hooked end of stem wire; see General Instructions for "Pointed" leaves on page 16.

6. Cut green silk ribbon into two equal lengths. Handling both as one, tie a bow around rosebud stem.

7. Glue rosebud to garter covering seam.

Lily of the Valley Set

Wedding Accessories

Lily of the Valley Set

Materials for Ring Pillow

$^3/_8$ yard of white cotton pique fabric
White sewing thread
1 yard of white decorative cording
20" of 1" white textured wired ribbon
$^3/_4$ yard of $^5/_8$" white wired ribbon
$^1/_4$ yard of $1^1/_2$" green wired ribbon
$1^7/_8$ yards of 18-gauge stem wire
Stuffing
Scissors
Quick tack fabric glue
Tacky glue or hot glue gun and glue sticks

Directions

1. Cut two 8" x 10" pieces of white pique fabric. Baste piping to wrong side of one piece. With right sides facing, sew a $^1/_4$" seam along all edges, sandwiching piping in seam and leaving a small opening for turning. Turn and stuff lightly. Slipstitch opening closed.

2. Wrap and glue 1" white textured wired ribbon around length of pillow with seam at center front.

3. Cut eleven 1" lengths from $^5/_8$" white wired ribbon. Make 11 lilies of the valley; see General Instructions for "Lilies of the Valley" on page 15.

4. With remaining $^5/_8$" white wired ribbon, tie a bow around lily bouquet.

5. Glue bouquet to pillow covering seam.

6. Put a drop of glue on each corner of green wired ribbon length. Fold corners toward center, making a point. Pinch ribbon length just off center, forming two leaves. Glue to leaves to pillow covering base of bouquet.

Materials for White Garter

$^3/_4$ yard of $1^1/_2$" white-mesh wired ribbon
$^3/_4$ yard of 1" white textured wired ribbon
$^3/_4$ yard of $^1/_4$" white satin ribbon
$^3/_4$ yard of $^1/_2$" white satin ribbon
$^3/_8$ yard of $^1/_4$" elastic
White sewing thread
$^3/_8$ yard of $^5/_8$" white wired ribbon
3" of $1^1/_2$" green wired ribbon
$^3/_4$ yard of 18-gauge stem wire
Scissors
Quick tack fabric glue
Tacky glue or hot glue gun and glue sticks

Directions

1. Remove wire from one long edge of textured and mesh wired ribbon. Overlap the wireless edges with the textured ribbon on top; topstitch. Place $^1/_4$" white satin ribbon over seam on right side. Topstitch.

2. Place $^1/_2$" white satin ribbon on wrong side of mesh wired ribbon, $1^1/_2$" from long wired edge. Sew along top and bottom edges, making a casing for elastic. With wrong sides facing, stitch short ends together, leaving casing open. Feed elastic through casing. Stitch ends together.

3. Cut five 1" lengths from $^5/_8$" white wired ribbon. Make five lilies of the valley; see General Instructions for "Lilies of the Valley" on page 15.

4. Cut green wired ribbon into two equal lengths. Make two pointed leaves, attaching to stem wire; see General Instructions for "Pointed" leaves on page 16.

5. Tie remaining length of $^5/_8$" white wired ribbon around lilies and leaves. Fold and glue raw short corners back, making diagonal finished ends. Glue bouquet to garter covering seam.

Chapter Four

Straw Garden Hat, Gloves & Wire Basket

Garden Accessories

Straw Garden Hat, Gloves & Wire Basket

Materials for Hat

One purchased straw hat
1 yard of $^1/_4$" green cord
10" of 1" red wired ribbon
4" of $1^1/_2$" black wired ribbon
12" of $1^1/_2$" plaid wired ribbon
24" of 5/8" yellow wired ribbon
2" of 1" brown wired ribbon
$^1/_4$ yard of $1^1/_2$" green wired ribbon
12" of 18-gauge stem wire
A small amount of stuffing
Brown sewing thread
Fabric paints: black and red
Paintbrush
Scissors
Quick tack fabric glue
Tacky glue or hot glue gun and glue sticks

Directions

1. Paint black dots on red and red dots on black wired ribbon. When dry, cut each into 2" lengths. Make seven berries; see General Instructions for "Berries" on page 18.

2. Cut $1^1/_2$" green wired ribbon into six $1^1/_2$" lengths. Make six pointed leaves; see General Instructions for "Pointed" leaves on page 16.

3. Cut sixteen $1^1/_2$" lengths from $^5/_8$" yellow wired ribbon. Cut two 1" lengths from brown wired ribbon. Make two eight-petaled sunflowers; see General Instructions for "Daisies" on page 12.

4. Wrap and glue $^1/_4$" green cord around straw hat in a wavy-lined circle; see photo.

5. Cut stem wire into four 3" lengths. Curl each length of stem wire into tight coils.

6. Fold and glue corners back on raw ends of plaid ribbon length, forming diagonal finished ends. Tie ribbon length into a bow. Glue bow to front of hat over cord.

7. Glue sunflowers on each side of bow. Glue berries, leaves, and coils as desired around hat over cord.

Materials for Gloves

One pair of purchased yellow cotton gloves
$^1/_4$ yard of green rattail
4" of 1" red wired ribbon
2" of $1^1/_2$" black wired ribbon
3" of $^1/_2$" green wired ribbon
3" of 18-gauge stem wire
A small amount of stuffing
Fabric paints: black and red
Paintbrush
Scissors
Quick tack fabric glue
Tacky glue or hot glue gun and glue sticks

Directions

1. Paint black dots on red and red dots on black wired ribbon. When dry, cut ribbon into 2" lengths. Make three berries; see General Instructions for "Berries" on page 18.

2. Cut $^1/_2$" green wired ribbon into three 1" lengths. Make three pointed leaves; see General Instructions for "Pointed" leaves on page 16.

3. Shape and glue green rattail to front of one glove, forming a stem; see photo.

4. Curl length of stem wire into a tight coil.

5. Glue berries, leaves, and coils as desired to glove over rattail.

Materials for Wire Basket

One purchased wire basket
$^1/_2$ yard of $2^5/_8$" white wired ribbon
1 yard" of $^1/_2$" white wired ribbon
$16^1/_2$" of $1^1/_2$" ombre green to white wired ribbon
12" of 18-gauge stem wire
Scissors
Quick tack fabric glue
Tacky glue or hot glue gun and glue sticks

Directions

1. Weave $2^5/_8$" white wired ribbon through bottom of wire basket.

2. Weave $^1/_2$" white wired ribbon through sides and handle of wire basket.

3. Cut $1^1/_2$" ombre wired ribbon into eleven $1^1/_2$" lengths. Make eleven pointed leaves; see General Instructions for "Pointed" leaves on page 16.

4. Cut four 3" lengths of stem wire. Curl each length of stem wire into a tight coil.

5. Glue leaves and coils as desired to wire basket.

Garden Accessories

Garden Green Jeans

Materials

One pair of purchased green overall shorts
5/8 yard of green rattail
4" of 1" red wired ribbon
14" of 1 1/2" plaid wired ribbon
1 yard of 5/8" yellow wired ribbon
3" of 1" brown wired ribbon
1 1/2" of 1 1/2" green wired ribbon
4" of 1/2" green wired ribbon
9" of 18-gauge stem wire
A small amount of stuffing
Brown sewing thread
Black fabric paint
Paintbrush
Scissors
Quick tack fabric glue
Tacky glue or hot glue gun and glue sticks

Directions

1. Paint black dots on red wired ribbon. When dry, cut into 2" lengths. Make two berries; see General Instructions for "Berries" on page 18.

2. Cut 1/2" green wired ribbon into four 1" lengths. From 1/2" and 1 1/2" green wired ribbon lengths, make five pointed leaves; see General Instructions for "Pointed" leaves on page 16.

3. Cut twenty-four 1 1/2" lengths from 5/8" yellow wired ribbon. Cut three 1" lengths from brown wired ribbon. Make three eight-petaled sunflowers; see General Instructions for "Daisies" on page 12.

4. Cut rattail into two 6" lengths and one 12" length. Shape and glue 6" lengths to bib of overalls, forming stems; see photo. Glue 12" length along top and one side edge of bib, forming a curvy vine; see photo.

5. Cut stem wire into four 3" lengths. Curl each length of stem wire into tight coils.

6. Glue sunflowers to tops of stems. Glue large pointed leaf to stem. Glue berries, leaves, and coils as desired to bib on vine.

7. Cut plaid wired ribbon into two 6" lengths and two 1" lengths. On one 6" length, overlap and glue raw ends, forming a tube. Fold 1" length in thirds. Wrap and glue 1" length around center of tube, covering seam and forming bow. Repeat with remaining lengths of ribbon to make two bows. Glue each bow to strap ends on overalls.

Canvas Hat, Gloves & Utility Bag

Garden Accessories

Canvas Hat, Gloves & Utility Bag

Materials for Hat

One purchased canvas hat
15" of $1^1/_2$" red wired ribbon
$7^1/_2$" of $1^1/_2$" yellow wired ribbon
6" of $1^1/_2$" green wired ribbon
6" of green rattail
Scissors
Quick tack fabric glue
Tacky glue or hot glue gun and glue sticks

Directions

1. Cut red wired ribbon into ten $1^1/_2$" lengths. Cut yellow wired ribbon into five $1^1/_2$" lengths. Make three nasturtiums; see General Instructions for "Nasturtiums" on page 15.

2. Cut green wired ribbon into three 2" lengths. Make three octagon leaves; see General Instructions for "Octagon" leaves on page 17.

3. On front of hat, glue brim up to side of hat. Cut rattail into two equal lengths. Shape and glue lengths to front side of hat, forming stems.

4. Glue one nasturtium on top of each stem. Glue remaining nasturtium on brim. Glue leaves to hat as desired.

Materials for Gloves

One pair of purchased canvas gloves
$7^1/_2$" of $1^1/_2$" red wired ribbon
2" of $1^1/_2$" green wired ribbon
Scissors
Quick tack fabric glue
Tacky glue or hot glue gun and glue sticks

Directions

1. Cut red wired ribbon into five $1^1/_2$" lengths. Make a nasturtium; see General Instructions for "Nasturtiums" on page 15.

2. Make an octagon leaf; see General Instructions for "Octagon" leaves on page 17.

3. Glue nasturtium and leaf to wrist of glove.

Materials for Utility Bag

One purchased canvas utility bag
7 1/2" of 1 1/2" red wired ribbon
7/8 yard of 1 1/2" yellow wired ribbon
8" of 1 1/2" green wired ribbon
12" of green rattail
Scissors
Quick tack fabric glue
Tacky glue or hot glue gun and glue sticks

Directions

1. Cut red wired ribbon into five 1 1/2" lengths. Cut yellow wired ribbon into twenty 1 1/2" lengths. Make five nasturtiums; see General Instructions for "Nasturtiums" on page 15.

2. Cut green wired ribbon into four 2" lengths. Make four octagon leaves; see General Instructions for "Octagon" leaves on page 17.

3. Cut rattail into four 3" lengths. Shape and glue three lengths to center front of bag, forming stems. Glue remaining length on top edge of bag, 3" from side edge.

4. Glue yellow nasturtiums to tops of each stem. Glue three leaves to center of bag around stems and flowers. Glue remaining nasturtium beside a leaf. Glue remaining leaf beside yellow nasturtium on top edge of bag.

Chapter Five

Country Christmas

Wreath & Bookmark

Country Christmas

Wreath & Bookmark

Materials for Wreath

One small vine wreath
3" of $1^1/_2$" green wired ribbon
1" of 1" red wired ribbon
3" section of novelty Christmas ribbon
A small amount of stuffing
Red sewing thread
9" of thin gold cord
Scissors
Quick tack fabric glue
Tacky glue or hot glue gun and glue sticks

Directions

1. On section of novelty Christmas ribbon, cut 1" up from center on one end. Fold and glue inside edges to long wired edges, making a V-shape; see photo. Repeat on opposite end.

2. Glue section of novelty Christmas ribbon across center of wreath.

3. Cut dark green wired ribbon into two equal lengths. Make two pointed leaves; see General Instructions for "Pointed" leaves on page 16.

4. Cut red wired ribbon into three 1" lengths. Form three pea-sized balls of stuffing and place one in center of each red ribbon length.

5. Gather ribbon around each ball and wrap with thread, making three holly berries. Cut away excess ribbon, being careful not to cut through thread.

6. Glue leaves and holly berry to wreath just above section of novelty Christmas ribbon.

7. Tie or glue ends of gold cord to top of wreath for hanger.

Materials for Bookmark

$10^1/_2$" of $1^1/_2$" red wired ribbon
$1^1/_2$" of $1^1/_2$" dark green wired ribbon
A small amount of stuffing
Red sewing thread
3" of 18-gauge stem wire
Scissors
Quick tack fabric glue
Tacky glue or hot glue gun and glue sticks

Directions

1. Cut $8^1/_2$" from red wired ribbon. Fold and glue one short end forward $^1/_8$". Fold again $1^1/_2$"; pinch and glue together. On opposite end, cut 1" up from center. Fold and glue inside edges to long wired edges, making a V-shape; see photo.

2. Make a pointed leaf from dark green wired ribbon and attach to stem wire; see General Instructions for "Pointed" leaves on page 16.

3. Cut remaining red wired ribbon into two 1" lengths. Form two pea-sized balls of stuffing, and place one in center of each red ribbon length.

4. Gather ribbon around each ball and wrap with thread, making three holly berries. Cut away excess ribbon, being careful not to cut through thread.

5. Glue leaf and holly berries to pinched area of bookmark, wrapping stems around bookmark to secure.

Country Christmas

Candle Clips & Snowman

Materials for Candle Clips

Purchased gold candle clips
24" of 1" red wired ribbon
24" of 1" gold-mesh wired ribbon
6" of $1\frac{1}{2}$" dark green wired ribbon
Scissors
Quick tack fabric glue
Tacky glue or hot glue gun and glue sticks

Directions

1. Glue one end of the red wired ribbon to the candleholder part of one clip. Wrap ribbon around candleholder loosely, folding edges and shaping to form bud; see photo.

2. Continue wrapping and shaping entire length of ribbon, forming a rose. Glue edges under the candleholder.

3. Cut dark green wired ribbon into two $1\frac{1}{2}$" lengths. Make two pointed leaves; see General Instructions for "Pointed" leaves on page 16.

4. Glue leaves to candle clip under rose.

5. Repeat Steps 1–4 using gold-mesh ribbon.

Materials for Snowman

$\frac{3}{8}$ yard of $2\frac{5}{8}$" white wired ribbon
6" of $1\frac{1}{2}$" white wired ribbon
6" of $\frac{5}{8}$" dark red wired ribbon
4" of $1\frac{1}{2}$ " dark green wired ribbon
Stuffing
Two artificial black stamens
Two small twigs
Metallic-gold paint
Paintbrush
Scissors
Quick tack fabric glue
Tacky glue or hot glue gun and glue sticks

Directions

1. Paint twigs gold; let dry.

2. Cut a $7\frac{1}{2}$" length of $2\frac{5}{8}$" white ribbon. Overlap and glue raw ends, forming a tube. Gather one long edge, forming a cup; glue. Stuff moderately. Gather and glue remaining long edge, forming snowman's lower section. Repeat with remaining $2\frac{5}{8}$" white wired ribbon, forming snowman's upper body, and $1\frac{1}{2}$" white wired ribbon, forming snowman's head. Glue head and lower body to either ends of upper body.

3. Ravel ends of $\frac{5}{8}$" dark red wired ribbon, making a scarf. Tie scarf around neck of snowman.

4. Overlap and glue raw ends of $1\frac{1}{2}$" dark green wired ribbon, forming a tube. Gather one long edge, forming a cup; glue. Fold back opposite long edge, forming cuff of hat. Glue hat on head.

5. Glue gold twigs to upper body for arms. Glue stamens to upper body for buttons.

Poinsettia Purse

Country Christmas

Poinsettia Purse

Materials for Poinsettia Purse

1/4 yard of dark green velvet
Green sewing thread
1/4 yard of red silk
1 1/2 yards of 1/8" gold trim
One small gold tassel
One snap set or Velcro fasteners
8 artificial gold stamens
12" of 1" dark red wired ribbon
15 3/4" of 5/8" dark red wired ribbon
1 1/2" of 1 1/2" dark green wired ribbon
Scissors
Quick tack fabric glue
Tacky glue or hot glue gun and glue sticks

Directions

1. Make purse pattern on pages 82 and 83. From green velvet, cut one purse. From red silk, cut one purse for lining.

2. Turn both raw ends of 1" dark red wired ribbon under 1/8". Pleat ribbon into a 4 1/2" length. With pleats toward center of green velvet piece, baste ribbon to right side of flap.

3. With right sides facing and edges aligned, stitch green velvet and red silk pieces together with a 1/4" seam, sandwiching pleated ribbon in seam and leaving a small opening for turning. Turn. Slipstitch opening closed.

4. Fold straight end over 4 1/4" with velvet facing; see Diagram. Stitch together along side edges. Turn.

5. Beginning and ending at point of flap, glue gold trim along edges of flap to side seams, making handle.

6. Glue gold tassel to point of flap, covering ends of trim. Attach snap set or Velcro fasteners on inside of flap.

7. Cut two 1 1/2" lengths of 5/8" dark red ribbon. Overlap lengths and glue long edges together. Fold and glue corners on one end back, forming a point. Pinch and glue the opposite end, forming a petal. Repeat to make three petals.

8. Cut three 1 1/4" lengths and three 1" lengths of 5/8" dark red wired ribbon. Fold and glue corners on one end of each length back, forming a point. Pinch and glue opposite ends, forming six petals.

9. Make a pointed leaf from dark green wired ribbon ; see General Instructions for "Pointed" leaves on page 16.

10. Glue 1" petals to stamen, next glue 1 1/4" petals, then overlapped petals, forming a poinsettia; see photo. Glue pointed leaf to underside of poinsettia.

11. Glue poinsettia to center front of purse flap.

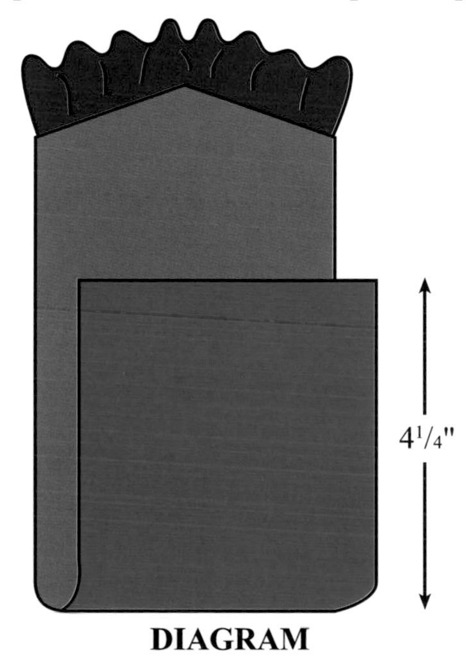

DIAGRAM

PURSE PATTERN
(Match dots to complete pattern)

PURSE PATTERN
(Match dots to complete pattern)

Merry Christmas
love the giver

Country Christmas

Angel Ornaments

Materials for White Angel

28" of 1" white textured wired ribbon
10" of $2^5/_8$" white wired ribbon
6" of $1^1/_2$" white wired ribbon
6" of $1^1/_2$" white-mesh wired ribbon
3" section of novelty Christmas ribbon
White sewing thread
Stuffing
Silver floral hair
6" of stem wire
Metallic-gold paint
Paintbrush
Toothpick
Scissors
Quick tack fabric glue
Tacky glue or hot glue gun and glue sticks

Directions

1. Paint stem wire gold; let dry.

2. Overlap and glue raw ends of $2^5/_8$" white ribbon, forming a tube. Gather one long edge, forming a cup, but do not glue.

3. Cut a 16" length of 1" white textured wired ribbon. Fold raw ends under $^1/_8$"; glue. Pull wire along one long edge, gathering ribbon to fit straight edge of tube; glue.

4. Cut $1^1/_2$" white wired ribbon into two equal lengths. Overlap and glue long edges, forming a 3" x 3" piece. Form a golf ball-sized ball of stuffing and place in center of ribbon.

5. Gather ribbon around ball and wrap with thread, making angel's head. Place head, gathered side down, into the gathers of the $2^5/_8$" white ribbon tube. Glue securely.

6. Cut two 3" lengths of 1" white textured wired ribbon. Overlap and glue long edges, forming a 3" x 2" piece. Overlap and glue raw ends of 3" x 2" piece, forming a tube. Gather and glue both long edges, forming angel's arm. Repeat to make two arms. Glue arms to sides of neck.

7. Fold raw ends of novelty Christmas ribbon back, making diagonal finished ends. Glue one end of ribbon to each arm. Shape floral hair into angel's hair. Glue on top of head. Form the gold stem wire into a halo and work into place along the back of the angel's head.

8. Fold raw ends of mesh wired ribbon back $^1/_8$"; glue. While glue is still pliable, place a round toothpick at an angle against the corner on the raw folded-edge side of the ribbon; see diagram on page 10. Roll ribbon around toothpick between thumb and forefinger one or two revolutions. Repeat on opposite end. Glue and pinch ribbon at center. Glue pinched center to back of angel at neck.

Materials for Gold Angel

12" of 1" gold plaid wired ribbon
10" of $2^5/_8$" gold plaid wired ribbon
6" of $1^1/_2$" gold wired ribbon
6" of $1^1/_2$" gold-mesh wired ribbon
3" section of novelty Christmas ribbon
Gold sewing thread
Stuffing
Gold floral hair
6" of stem wire
Metallic-gold paint
Paintbrush
Toothpick
Scissors
Quick tack fabric glue
Tacky glue or hot glue gun and glue sticks

Directions

Follow directions for making White Angel omitting Step 3.

Chapter Six

Wildflower Heart Sachets

Home Decor

Wildflower Heart Sachets

Materials for Heart Sachets

$^{1}/_{2}$ yard of white fabric
White sewing thread
$1^{1}/_{4}$ yard of $^{1}/_{4}$" trim in desired color
Potpourri
14" of $^{5}/_{8}$" ombre violet to green wired ribbon
16" of $^{5}/_{8}$" ombre blue to white wired ribbon
Four yellow artificial stamens
10" of 1" ombre pink to white wired ribbon
2" of 1" pink and blue woven wired ribbon
2" of 1" white wired ribbon
6" of $1^{1}/_{2}$" green wired ribbon
4" of $^{5}/_{8}$" green wired ribbon
$1^{3}/_{4}$ yard of 18-gauge stem wire
A small amount of stuffing
Scissors
Quick tack fabric glue
Tacky glue or hot glue gun and glue sticks

Directions

1. Make heart patterns on pages 90 and 91. From white fabric, cut two of each heart. With right sides facing and edges aligned, stitch two pieces together, leaving a small opening in seam. Turn. Stuff with potpourri. Slipstitch opening closed. Repeat for all hearts.

2. Cut the stem wire into 3" lengths. Cut the $1^{1}/_{2}$" green wired ribbon into four $1^{1}/_{2}$" lengths. Make two heart-shaped leaves and two pointed leaves, attaching to stem wire; see General Instructions for "Heart-Shaped" and "Pointed" leaves on page 16.

3. Cut the ombre violet to green wired ribbon into fourteen 1" lengths. Make two violets and two violet buds, see General Instructions for "Violets" on page 11.

4. To make forget-me-nots, cut the ombre blue to white wired ribbon into sixteen 1" lengths. Make four violets, gluing one stamen to hooked end of stem wire, see General Instructions for "Violets" on page 11.

5. Cut the ombre pink to white wired ribbon into five 2" lengths. On one length, overlap and glue raw ends, forming a tube. Gather and glue one long end around length of stem wire. Repeat for remaining lengths. Fill three gathered tubes with stuffing. Gather and glue open long edges, forming puffs. On remaining gathered tubes, cut wire from open long edge and ravel the threads, creating a fringe.

6. Cut the $^{5}/_{8}$" green wired ribbon into four 1" lengths. Make two pointed leaves and two leaf caps, attaching caps to two puffs; see General Instructions for "Pointed" leaves and "Leaf Caps" on pages 16 and 18 respectively.

7. Bundle violets and two heart-shaped leaves together and glue to cleavage of small/medium heart. Cut a 9" length of trim. Knot each end and glue knots to top of heart on either side of cleavage.

8. Bundle forget-me-knots and two pointed leaves together and glue to cleavage of large heart. Cut an 18" length of trim. Knot each end and glue knots to top of heart on either side of cleavage.

9. Bundle the two puffs together and glue to cleavage of small heart. Cut a 6" length of trim. Knot each end and glue knots to top of heart on either side of cleavage.

10. Bundle remaining flowers and leaves together and glue to cleavage of medium/large heart. Cut a 12" length of trim. Knot each end and glue knots to top of heart on either side of cleavage.

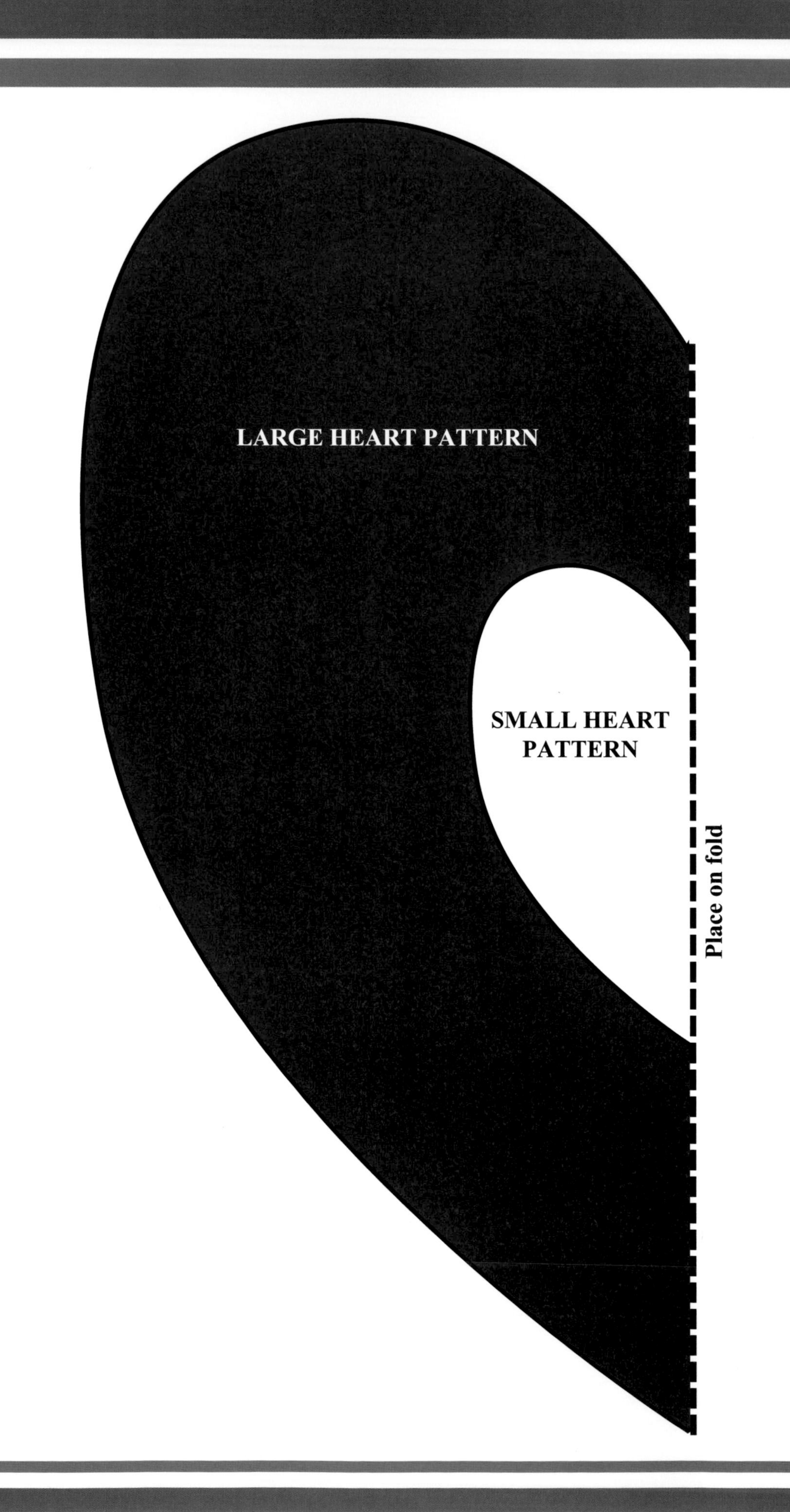
LARGE HEART PATTERN
SMALL HEART PATTERN
Place on fold

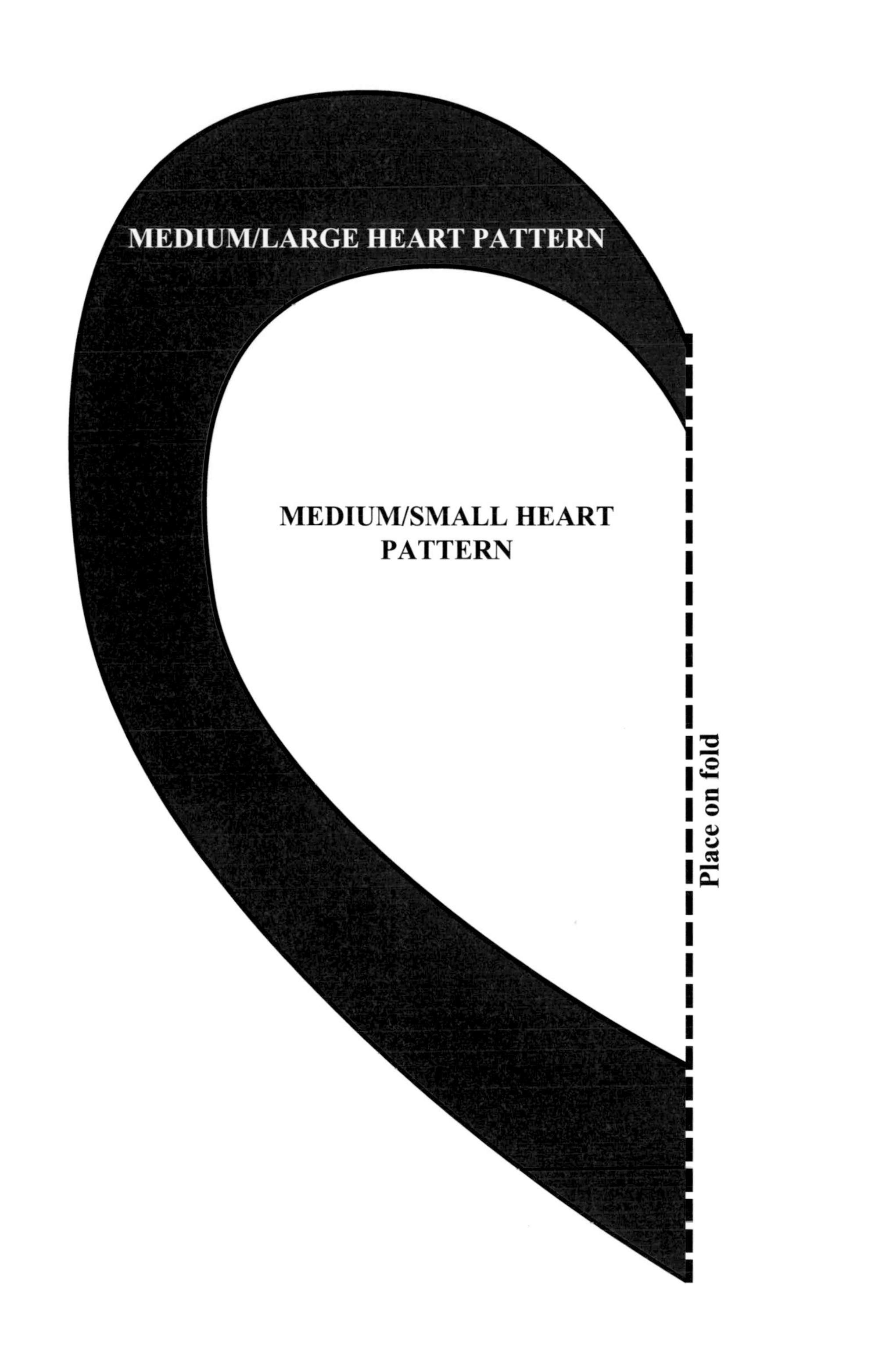
MEDIUM/LARGE HEART PATTERN
MEDIUM/SMALL HEART PATTERN
Place on fold

Framed Potted Plants

Home Decor

Framed Potted Plants

Materials for Geranium

12" x 12" piece of cream fabric
48" of $^{5}/_{8}$" ombre pink to white wired ribbon
12" of $1^{1}/_{2}$" green wired ribbon
7" of $2^{5}/_{8}$" brown wired ribbon
$^{1}/_{2}$ yard of green rattail
Scissors
Quick tack fabric glue
Tacky glue or hot glue gun and glue sticks

Directions

1. Cut ombre wired ribbon into three $3^{1}/_{2}$" lengths, three $2^{1}/_{2}$" lengths, three 2" lengths, and six 4" lengths. On one length, overlap and glue raw ends, forming a tube. Gather and glue the pink long edge, forming flowers. Repeat with all lengths. Lightly stuff the three 2" tubes. Gather and glue the remaining long edge, forming three buds.

2. Cut the green wired ribbon into six 2" lengths. Make six octagon leaves; see General Instructions for "Octagon" leaves on page 17.

3. Make a pot from brown wired ribbon; see General instructions for "Pots" on page 19. Glue pot to cream fabric, centered horizontally on lower third of fabric.

4. Cut rattail into two 5" lengths, two 3" lengths, and one 2" length. Glue rattail lengths to cream fabric with each end tucked inside rim of pot and shape to form stems; see photo.

5. Place and glue flowers and leaves to stems; see photo. Frame as desired.

Materials for Cyclamen

12" x 12" piece of cream fabric
$10^{1}/_{2}$" of $^{5}/_{8}$" ombre pink to red wired ribbon
$7^{1}/_{2}$" of $1^{1}/_{2}$" green wired ribbon
7" of $2^{5}/_{8}$" brown wired ribbon
12" of green rattail
Scissors
Quick tack fabric glue
Tacky glue or hot glue gun and glue sticks

Directions

1. Cut ombre wired ribbon into six $1^{3}/_{4}$" lengths. On one length, fold and glue one raw end of each length under $^{1}/_{8}$". Fold corners slightly on folded edge, forming a blunt point; glue. Pinch and glue opposite end, forming a petal. Repeat to make six petals.

2. With wrong sides facing, glue two petals together at pinched ends. Twist tops together, forming an elongated bud. With wrong sides facing, glue remaining petals together at pinched ends. Fold front petal forward and down.

3. Cut the green wired ribbon into six $1^{1}/_{2}$" lengths. Make five heart-shaped leaves; see General Instructions for "Heart-Shaped" leaves on page 16. With remaining length of ribbon, make a leaf cap, attaching to base of bud; see General Instructions for "Leaf Caps" on page 18.

4. Make a pot from brown wired ribbon; see General instructions for "Pots" on page 19. Glue pot to cream fabric, centered horizontally on lower third of fabric. Cut rattail into two 4" lengths, and two 2" lengths. Glue rattail lengths to cream fabric with each end tucked inside rim of pot and shape to form stems; see photo.

5. Place and glue flower, bud, and leaves to stems; see photo. Frame as desired.

Materials for Violets

12" x 12" piece of cream fabric
24" of 5/8" violet wired ribbon
1/4 yard of 1 1/2" green wired ribbon
7" of 2 5/8" brown wired ribbon
2 yards of 18-gauge stem wire
Scissors
Quick tack fabric glue
Tacky glue or hot glue gun and glue sticks

Directions

1. Cut violet wired ribbon into twenty-four 1" lengths. Make six violets, attaching to stem wire; see General Instructions for "Violets" on page 11.

2. Cut the green wired ribbon into six 1 1/2" lengths. Make six heart-shaped leaves, attaching to stem wire; see General Instructions for "Heart-Shaped" leaves on page 16.

3. Make a pot from brown wired ribbon; see General instructions for "Pots" on page 19. Glue pot to cream fabric, centered horizontally on lower third of fabric.

4. Glue violets and leaves to cream fabric with each end of wire tucked inside rim of pot; see photo. Frame as desired.

Materials for Shamrock

12" x 12" piece of cream fabric
48" of 5/8" green wired ribbon
2" of 5/8" white wired ribbon
7" of 2 5/8" brown wired ribbon
2 1/4 yards of 18-gauge stem wire
Scissors
Quick tack fabric glue
Tacky glue or hot glue gun and glue sticks

Directions

1. Cut green wired ribbon into forty-eight 1" lengths. Make twelve shamrocks, attaching to stem wire; see General Instructions for "Violets" on page 11; shape small V-shapes on top edges of petals.

2. Overlap and glue raw ends of white wired ribbon length, forming a tube. Gather and glue one long edge around remaining stem wire, forming flower.

3. Make a pot from brown wired ribbon; see General instructions for "Pots" on page 19. Glue pot to cream fabric, centered horizontally on lower third of fabric.

4. Glue flower and shamrocks to cream fabric with each end of wire tucked inside rim of pot; see photo. Frame as desired.

Framed Potted Plants

Home Decor

Framed Potted Plants

Materials for Pansies

12" x 12" piece of cream fabric
28$^{3}/_{4}$" of 1$^{1}/_{2}$" wired ribbon in desired colors
(5$^{3}/_{4}$" per pansy)
3$^{3}/_{4}$" of 1$^{1}/_{2}$" green wired ribbon
7" of 2$^{5}/_{8}$" brown wired ribbon
48" of 18-gauge stem wire
Scissors
Quick tack fabric glue
Tacky glue or hot glue gun and glue sticks

Directions

1. Make five pansies and attach to stem wire; see General Instructions for "Pansies" on page 10.

2. Cut the green wired ribbon into three 1$^{1}/_{4}$" lengths. Make three pansy leaves, attaching to stem wire; see General Instructions for "Pansy" leaves on page 17.

3. Make a pot from brown wired ribbon; see General instructions for "Pots" on page 19. Glue pot to cream fabric, centered horizontally on lower third of fabric.

4. Glue pansies and leaves to cream fabric with each end of wire tucked inside rim of pot; see photo. Frame as desired.

Fancy Floral Sachets

Fancy Floral Sachets

Materials for Pansy Sachet

$^1/_4$ yard of green taffeta fabric
Green sewing thread
$^7/_8$ yard of $1^1/_2$" wired ribbon in desired colors ($5^3/_4$" per pansy)
6" of $1^1/_2$" green wired ribbon
8" of 1" wired ribbon in desired color
$1^3/_8$ yard of stem wire
One $1^1/_2$" pinback
Potpourri
Scissors
Quick tack fabric glue
Tacky glue or hot glue gun and glue sticks
Fabric pens: black and gold

Directions

1. Cut green taffeta into two 7" squares. With right sides facing and edges aligned, stitch squares together, leaving a small opening in one seam. Turn. Stuff moderately with potpourri. Slipstitch opening closed.

2. Make five pansies and attach to stem wire; see General Instructions for "Pansies" on page 10.

3. Cut green wired ribbon into three 2" lengths. Make three pansy leaves and attach to stem wire; see General Instructions for "Pansy" leaves on page 17.

4. Using the 8" length of 1" wired ribbon, fold one corner on one raw end so that the raw end is aligned with one long edge of ribbon. Repeat on opposite raw end, creating diagonal finished ends.

5. Bundle the pansies and pansy leaves together. Glue the pinback to the stems at the center of the bundle. Tie the bundle together with the 8" length of ribbon, securing the pinback in place. Pin the bouquet to the center of the sachet. With gold fabric pen write "Pansies for thoughts."

Materials for Violet Sachet

$^1/_4$ yard of purple taffeta fabric
Purple sewing thread
$1^3/_8$ yards of 1" violet wired ribbon
6" of $1^1/_2$" green wired ribbon
3 yards of stem wire
One $1^1/_2$" pinback
Potpourri
Scissors
Quick tack fabric glue
Tacky glue or hot glue gun and glue sticks
Gold fabric pen

Directions

1. Cut purple taffeta into two 7" squares. With right sides facing and edges aligned, stitch squares together, leaving a small opening in one seam. Turn. Stuff moderately with potpourri. Slipstitch opening closed.

2. Cut violet wired ribbon into thirty 1" lengths. Make six violets and two buds; see General Instructions for "Violets" on page 11.

3. Cut green wired ribbon into three 2" lengths. Make three heart-shaped leaves and attach to stem wire; see General Instructions for "Heart-Shaped" leaves on page 16.

4. Bundle the violets, buds, and leaves together. Glue the pinback to the stems at the center of the bundle.

5. Fold one corner of the remaining violet wired ribbon on one raw end so that the raw end is aligned with one long edge of ribbon. Repeat on opposite raw end, creating diagonal finished ends. Tie a bow around bundle, securing the pinback in place. Pin the bouquet to the center of the sachet. With gold fabric pen write "Violets for faithful-ness."

Home Decor

Country Throw Pillows

Materials for Beehive

12" x 12" pillow form
12" x 12" white pillow cover
2 1/2 yards of 1/4" gold cord
Metallic-gold floral hair
4 1/2" of 5/8" gold-mesh wired ribbon
5" of 1" yellow wired ribbon
12" of 5/8" white wired ribbon
8" of 18-gauge stem wire
A small amount of stuffing
Six black artificial stamens
Scissors
Quick tack fabric glue
Tacky glue or hot glue gun and glue sticks

Directions

1. Cut three 1" lengths from 1/4" cord. Set aside. Coil and glue remaining cord to pillow cover front, beginning 2" from bottom edge and gradually making smaller coils to resemble a beehive; see photo. Glue floral hair on top of beehive.

2. Cut twelve 1" lengths from white wired ribbon and two 1" lengths from yellow wired ribbon. Make two six-petaled daisies; see General Instructions for "Daisies" on page 12. Glue daisies to pillow cover front on each side of beehive.

3. From remaining ribbon and cord, make three bees; see General Instructions for "Bees" on page 19. Glue bees to pillow cover front above beehive.

7. Insert pillow form inside cover.

Home Decor

Country Throw Pillows

Materials for Strawberry Basket

12" x 12" pillow form
12" x 12" white pillow cover
1 3/4 yard of 1" brown wired ribbon
15" of 1 1/2" ombre pink to red wired ribbon
12" of 1 1/2" green wired ribbon
1" of 1" yellow wired ribbon
1 1/2" of 5/8" silver-mesh wired ribbon
4" of 5/8" white wired ribbon
Stuffing
1" of 1/4" cord
Six yellow artificial stamens
Two black artificial stamens
Pins
Scissors
Quick tack fabric glue
Tacky glue or hot glue gun and glue sticks

Directions

1. From brown wired ribbon, cut six 3 1/2" lengths, three 7" lengths, and one 8" length. Center and pin the 7" lengths horizontally 2 1/2" from bottom of pillow cover front. Weave the 3 1/2" lengths vertically through 7" lengths, forming basket. Turn all raw edges under and glue. Fold 8" length in half, forming a V-shape. Glue ends to top edge of basket, forming handle.

2. Cut pink wired ribbon into five 3" lengths. Make five berries; see General Instructions for "Berries" on page 18.

3. Cut green wired ribbon into eight 1 1/2" lengths. Make five leaf caps, attaching to tops of berries; see General Instructions for "Leaf Caps" on page 18. Make three octagon leaves from remaining lengths of ribbon; see General Instructions for "Octagon" leaves on page 17.

4. Cut four 1" lengths from 5/8" white wired ribbon. Make a flower; see General Instructions for "Violets" on page 11. Glue yellow stamens in center of flower. Glue flower, berries, and leaves on top edge of basket.

5. From remaining ribbon and cord, make a bee; see General Instructions for "Bees" on page 19. Glue bee to pillow cover front above basket.

6. Insert pillow form inside cover.

Home Decor

Country Throw Pillows

Materials for Briar Wreath

12" x 12" pillow form
12" x 12" black pillow cover
$\frac{5}{8}$ yard of brown rattail
12" of $1\frac{1}{2}$" green wired ribbon
10" of $1\frac{1}{2}$" black wired ribbon
10" of 1" red wired ribbon
4" of $\frac{5}{8}$" white wired ribbon
2" of 1" light green wired ribbon
12" of 18-gauge stem wire
Stuffing
Three white artificial stamens
Fabric paints: black and red
Paintbrush
Scissors
Quick tack fabric glue
Tacky glue or hot glue gun and glue sticks

Directions

1. Paint black dots on red and light green wired ribbons. Paint red dots on black wired ribbon. When dry, cut each into 2" lengths. Make eleven berries; see General Instructions for "Berries" on page 18.

2. Cut $1\frac{1}{2}$" green wired ribbon into eight $1\frac{1}{2}$" lengths. Make eight pointed leaves; see General Instructions for "Pointed" leaves on page 16.

3. Cut four 1" lengths from $\frac{5}{8}$" white wired ribbon. Make a briar flower; see General Instructions for "Violets" on page 11. Glue white stamens in center of flower.

4. Glue rattail to pillow cover front in a wavy-lined circle, 2" from outer edges; see photo.

5. Cut stem wire into four 3" lengths. Curl each length of stem wire into tight coils.

6. Glue berries, flower, leaves, and coils as desired to pillow cover front over rattail.

7. Insert pillow form inside cover.

Neglect
not the gift
that is in
thee

Home Decor

Country Throw Pillows

Materials for Gift Wreath

12" x 12" pillow form
12" x 12" white pillow cover
$^{5}/_{8}$ yard of green rattail
9" of 1" green wired ribbon
8" of $^{5}/_{8}$" ombre pink to white wired ribbon
2" each or of 1" black, red, and pink wired ribbon
6" of $^{5}/_{8}$" white wired ribbon
7" of 1" yellow wired ribbon
$5^{3}/_{4}$" of $1^{1}/_{2}$" wired ribbon in desired colors for pansy
8" of $^{5}/_{8}$" violet wired ribbon
12" of 18-gauge stem wire
Fabric paints: black and red
Gold fabric pen
Paintbrush
Scissors
Quick tack fabric glue
Tacky glue or hot glue gun and glue sticks

Directions

1. Paint black dots on red wired ribbon. Paint red dots on black wired ribbon. Let dry. Make three berries from red, black, and pink 1" wired ribbons; see General Instructions for "Berries" on page 18.

2. Cut green wired ribbon into six $1^{1}/_{2}$" lengths. Make five pointed leaves and one leaf cap, attaching to top of pink berry; see General Instructions for "Pointed" leaves and "Leaf Caps" on pages 16 and 18 respectively.

3. Cut one 1" length of yellow wired ribbon. Cut six 1" lengths of white wired ribbon. Make a six-petaled daisy; see General Instructions for "Daisies" on page 12.

4. Cut remaining yellow wired ribbon into 2" lengths. On one length, overlap and glue raw ends, forming a tube. Gather and glue one long edge, forming a cup. Repeat with remaining lengths.

5. Make a pansy from $1^{1}/_{2}$" wired ribbon, omitting stem wire; see General Instructions for "Pansies" on page 10.

6. Cut eight 1" lengths from $^{5}/_{8}$" violet wired ribbon. Make two violets; see General Instructions for "Violets" on page 11.

7. Glue rattail to pillow cover front in a wavy-lined circle, 3" from outer edges; see photo.

8. Cut stem wire into four 3" lengths. Curl each length of stem wire into tight coils.

9. Glue berries, flowers, leaves, and coils as desired to pillow cover front over rattail. Fold ends of ombre ribbon under. Tie ribbon into a bow and glue to bottom of wreath. With fabric pen write "Neglect not the gift that is in thee."

10. Insert pillow form inside cover.

Home Sweet Home

Home Decor

Country Throw Pillows

Materials for Bird House

12" x 12" pillow form
12" x 12" black pillow cover
12" of 2" ombre blue to brown wired ribbon
8" of 1" brown wired ribbon
5" of 1/2" white wired ribbon
Metallic-gold floral hair
1 yard of 1" gold decorative trim
Black fabric pen
Scissors
Quick tack fabric glue
Tacky glue or hot glue gun and glue sticks

Directions

1. Cut ombre wired ribbon into two equal lengths. Lay pieces side by side with blue edges touching. Fold and glue one raw end on each length under. Draw two 3/4" half circles at center, long blue edges of lengths. Cut out. Clip curved edges; fold under and glue. Fold top raw edges of each length back, making a pointed roof; see Diagram. Glue lengths to pillow cover front, 2" from bottom edge.

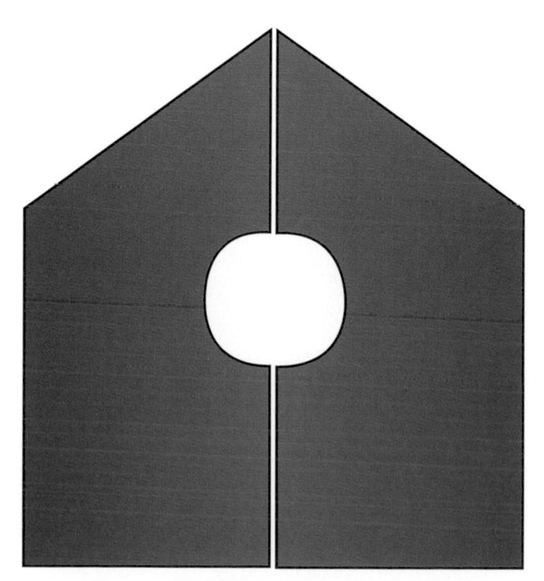

DIAGRAM

2. Fold raw ends of brown wired ribbon under. Glue ribbon over edges of roof.

3. Shape floral hair into a 1 1/2"-diameter nest. Glue nest to pillow cover front in circular hole on house.

4. Print "Home Sweet Home" on white wired ribbon, leaving 1" unprinted on each end. Glue raw ends under and glue ribbon length to house above bird nest.

5. Glue decorative trim to pillow cover front, 2" from all edges, framing bird house.

6. Insert pillow form inside cover.

Country Throw Pillows

Materials for Bird Nest

12" x 12" pillow form
12" x 12" black pillow cover
1/4 yard of 1" brown wired ribbon
6" of 1 1/2" ombre dark blue to blue wired ribbon
4 1/2" of 1 1/2" green wired ribbon
1/4 yard of 1/4" gold cord
Metallic-gold floral hair
1 yard of 1" gold decorative trim
A small amount of stuffing
Scissors
Quick tack fabric glue
Tacky glue or hot glue gun and glue sticks

Directions

1. Cut one 5 1/2" length and one 3 1/2" length of brown wired ribbon. Cut one 5" length and one 3" length of 1/4" cord. Wrap ribbons lengthwise around each piece of cord; glue. Fold and glue raw ends under. Glue seam sides down on pillow cover front as desired forming branches.

2. Shape floral hair into a 3 1/2"-diameter nest. Glue nest to pillow cover front over branches.

3. Cut ombre wired ribbon into two equal lengths. On one length, overlap and glue raw ends, forming a tube. Gather and glue one long edge, forming a cup. Stuff lightly. Gather and glue remaining long edge, forming robin egg. Repeat to make two robin eggs. Glue eggs inside nest.

4. Cut green wired ribbon into three 1 1/2" lengths. Make three pointed leaves; see General Instructions for "Pointed" leaves on page 16. Glue leaves to branches under nest.

5. Glue decorative trim to pillow cover front, 2" from all edges, framing bird nest

Home Decor

Four Seasons

Materials for Spring

10" x 10" piece of green velvet
1 yard of light green rattail
21" of 18-gauge stem wire
4" of $^5/_8$" violet wired ribbon
7" of 1" ombre pink to white wired ribbon
6" of 1" ombre blue to white wired ribbon
3" of 1" ombre green to white wired ribbon
7" of $^1/_2$" white wired ribbon
7" of $^1/_2$" green wired ribbon
9" of $^5/_8$" white wired ribbon
5" of 1" yellow wired ribbon
Yellow sewing thread
A small amount of stuffing
Black fabric paint
Paintbrush
Scissors
Quick tack fabric glue
Tacky glue or hot glue gun and glue sticks

Directions

1. Cut violet wired ribbon into four 1" lengths. Make a violet; see General Instructions for "Violets" on page 11.

2. Cut ombre pink wired ribbon into four 1" lengths. Make two rosebuds; see General Instructions for "Rosebuds" on page 14.

3. Cut blue ombre wired ribbon into three 2" lengths. On one length, overlap and glue raw ends, forming a tube. Gather and glue one long edge, forming a cup. Repeat to make three flower cups.

4. Cut $^1/_2$" white wired ribbon into one 2" length and five 1" lengths. Make a daffodil; see General Instructions for "Daffodils" on page 13.

5. Cut $^1/_2$" green wired ribbon into seven 1" lengths. Make seven pointed leaves; see General Instructions for "Pointed" leaves on page 16.

6. Cut $^5/_8$" white wired ribbon into three 1" lengths. Make three lilies of the valley, attaching each to a 3" length of stem wire; see General Instructions for "Lilies of the Valley" on page 15.

7. Cut remaining $^5/_8$" white wired ribbon into six 1" lengths. Cut one 1" length of yellow wired ribbon. Make a six-petaled daisy; see General Instructions for "Daisies" on page 12.

8. Cut remaining yellow wired ribbon into two 2" lengths. On one length, overlap and glue raw ends, forming a tube. Gather and glue one long edge, forming a cup. Repeat to make two flower cups.

9. Cut a 1" length from ombre green wired ribbon. Make a heart-shaped leaf; see General Instructions for "Heart-Shaped" leaves on page 16. Paint black dots on remaining ombre green wired ribbon. When dry, make a berry; see General Instructions for "Berries" on page 18.

10. Glue rattail to velvet piece in a wavy-lined circle, 2" from outer edges; see photo.

11. Cut stem wire into four 3" lengths. Curl each length of stem wire into tight coils.

12. Glue berry, flowers, leaves, and coils as desired to rattail circle on velvet piece. Copy angel pattern on page 114. Color as desired and glue to center of velvet piece.

ANGEL PATTERN FOR SPRING

PUTNAM

Home Decor

Four Seasons

Materials for Summer

10" x 10" piece of green velvet
1 yard of light green rattail
15" of 18-gauge stem wire
$5\frac{3}{4}$" of $1\frac{1}{2}$" ombre rose to cream wired ribbon
4" of $\frac{5}{8}$" violet wired ribbon
7" of $\frac{5}{8}$" white wired ribbon
7" of 1" ombre pink to white wired ribbon
8" of 1" ombre blue to white wired ribbon
6" of 1" ombre red to white wired ribbon
3" of 1" ombre purple to green wired ribbon
6" of 1" ombre green to white wired ribbon
6" of $\frac{1}{2}$" green wired ribbon
6" of $\frac{5}{8}$" pink wired ribbon
6" of $\frac{5}{8}$" yellow wired ribbon
2" of 1" bronze wired ribbon
2" of 1" yellow wired ribbon
1" of $\frac{1}{2}$" red wired ribbon
Brown sewing thread
A small amount of stuffing
Black fabric paint
Paintbrush
Scissors
Quick tack fabric glue
Tacky glue or hot glue gun and glue sticks

Directions

1. From ombre rose to cream wired ribbon, make a pansy; see General Instructions for "Pansies" on page 10.

2. Cut violet and white $\frac{5}{8}$" wired ribbon into four 1" lengths each. Make two violets; see General Instructions for "Violets" on page 11.

3. Cut $\frac{5}{8}$" white wired ribbon into three 1" lengths. Make three lilies of the valley, attaching each to a 3" length of stem wire; see General Instructions for "Lilies of the Valley" on page 15.

4. Cut ombre pink wired ribbon into four 1" lengths. Make two rosebuds; see General Instructions for "Rosebuds" on page 14.

5. Cut blue ombre wired ribbon into four 2" lengths. On one length, overlap and glue raw ends, forming a tube. Gather and glue one long edge, forming a cup. Repeat to make four flower cups.

6. Cut ombre purple wired ribbon into one 1" length and one 2" length. Cut one 1" length of rattail. Make a bee; see General Instructions for "Bees" on page 19.

7. Cut $\frac{1}{2}$" green wired ribbon into six 1" lengths. From four lengths, make four pointed leaves; see General Instructions for "Pointed" leaves on page 16. From remaining lengths, make two leaf caps, attaching to bases of rosebuds; see General Instructions for "Leaf Caps" on page 18.

8. Cut pink and yellow $\frac{5}{8}$" wired ribbon into six 1" lengths each. Cut two 1" lengths of bronze wired ribbon. Make two six-petaled daisies; see General Instructions for "Daisies" on page 12.

9. Overlap and glue raw ends of 1" yellow wired ribbon length, forming a tube. Gather and glue one long edge, forming a cup. Repeat with $\frac{1}{2}$" red wired ribbon to make two flower cups.

10. Paint black dots on ombre red wired ribbon. When dry, cut into three 2" lengths and make three berries; see General Instructions for "Berries" on page 18.

11. Cut ombre green wired ribbon into six 1" lengths. From three lengths, make three heart-shaped leaves; see General Instructions for "Heart-Shaped" leaves on page 16. From remaining lengths, make three leaf caps, attaching to tops of berries; see General Instructions for "Leaf Caps" on page 18.

12. Glue rattail to velvet piece in a wavy-lined circle, 2" from outer edges; see photo.

13. Cut stem wire into five 3" lengths. Curl each length of stem wire into tight coils.

14. Glue berries, bee, flowers, leaves, and coils as desired to rattail circle on velvet piece. Copy angel pattern below. Color as desired and glue to center of velvet piece.

Pansies for thoughts

Home Decor

Four Seasons

Materials for Autumn

10" x 10" piece of green velvet
1 yard of $^1/_2$" green cord
15" of 18-gauge brown stem wire
4" of 1" ombre yellow to brown wired ribbon
5" of 1" brown wired ribbon
4" of 1" bronze wired ribbon
4" of 1" red wired ribbon
Nine 2" lengths of 1" ombre wired ribbon in autumn shades
2" of 1" yellow wired ribbon
1$^1/_2$" of $^5/_8$" gold-mesh wired ribbon
5" of $^5/_8$" white wired ribbon
3" of 1" ombre red to orange wired ribbon
3" of 1" green wired ribbon
Yellow sewing thread
A small amount of stuffing
Black fabric paint
Paintbrush
Scissors
Quick tack fabric glue
Tacky glue or hot glue gun and glue sticks

Directions

1. Cut 1" ombre yellow to brown wired ribbon into two equal lengths. On one length, overlap and glue raw ends, forming a tube. Gather and glue one long edge, forming a cup. Fill with stuffing. Gather and glue remaining long edge, forming acorn. Repeat with remaining length. Cut 1" brown wired ribbon into two equal lengths. Fold one long edge forward and wrap around one acorn; glue. Pinch and glue ends. Repeat on other acorn.

2. Cut bronze wired ribbon into four 1" lengths. Make two rosebuds; see General Instructions for "Rosebuds" on page 14.

3. Paint black dots on red wired ribbon. When dry, cut into two equal lengths. Make two berries; see General Instructions for "Berries" on page 18.

4. On one 2" length of autumn-shaded ribbon, overlap and glue raw ends, forming a tube. Gather and glue one long edge, forming a cup. Repeat to make nine flower cups. On five cups, gather and glue remaining long edge, forming closed flower cups.

5. Cut a 1" length from 1" yellow wired ribbon. Cut one 1" length of green cord. Make a bee; see General Instructions for "Bees" on page 19.

6. Cut $^5/_8$" white wired ribbon into five 1" lengths. Make a five-petaled daisy; see General Instructions for "Daisies" on page 12.

7. Cut ombre red to orange wired ribbon into two equal lengths. Make two heart-shaped leaves; see General Instructions for "Heart-Shaped" leaves on page 16.

8. Cut 1" green wired ribbon into three 1" lengths. Make three pointed leaves; see General Instructions for "Pointed" leaves on page 16.

9. Glue cord to velvet piece in a wavy-lined circle, 2" from outer edges; see photo.

10. Cut stem wire into five 3" lengths. Curl each length of stem wire into tight coils.

11. Glue berries, bee, flowers, leaves, and coils as desired to cord circle on velvet piece. Copy angel pattern on page 120. Color as desired and glue to center of velvet piece.

ANGEL PATTERN FOR AUTUMN

SECRETS

Home Decor

Four Seasons

Materials for Winter

10" x 10" piece of green velvet
1 yard of 1/2" green cord
1/4 yard of 18-gauge brown stem wire
1/4 yard of 1" red wired ribbon
24" of 1 1/2" dark green wired ribbon
Red sewing thread
A small amount of stuffing
Scissors
Quick tack fabric glue
Tacky glue or hot glue gun and glue sticks

Directions

1. Cut dark green wired ribbon into twelve 2" lengths. Make 12 pointed leaves; see General Instructions for "Pointed" leaves on page 16.

2. Cut red wired ribbon into nine 1" lengths. Form nine pea-sized balls of stuffing and place one in center of each red ribbon length.

3. Gather ribbon around each ball and wrap with thread, making nine holly berries. Cut away excess ribbon, being careful not to cut through thread.

4. Glue cord to velvet piece in a wavy-lined circle, 2" from outer edges; see photo.

5. Cut stem wire into five 3" lengths. Curl each length of stem wire into tight coils.

6. Glue leaves, holly berries, and coils as desired to cord circle on velvet piece. Copy angel pattern on page 123. Color as desired and glue to center of velvet piece.

ANGEL PATTERN FOR WINTER

Home Decor

Floral Pillows

Materials for Foxglove

12" x 12" pillow form
12" x 12" white pillow cover
10" of 1 1/2" ombre green to pink wired ribbon
15" of 1" ombre green to pink wired ribbon
12" of 1 1/2" green wired ribbon
Black fabric pen
Scissors
Quick tack fabric glue
Tacky glue or hot glue gun and glue sticks

Directions

1. Cut the 1 1/2" ombre wired ribbon into four 2 1/2" lengths. On one length, overlap and glue raw ends, forming a tube. Gather and glue green long edge, forming a cup. With fabric pen, make dots on inside of gathered tube and fold edge opposite seam back 1/8". Repeat to make four tubes.

2. Cut the 1" ombre wired ribbon into two 2 1/2" lengths, and five 2" lengths. Make seven gathered tubes as in Step 1, omitting dots inside tubes. Fill three gathered tubes with stuffing. Gather and glue remaining long edge, forming three stuffed buds.

3. Cut the green wired ribbon into two 2 1/2" lengths, two 2" lengths, and two 1 1/2" lengths. Make six pointed leaves; see General Instructions for "Pointed" leaves on page 16.

4. Glue rattail to pillow cover front, 2" from bottom edge, shaping to form a stem. Glue a stuffed bud at top of stem. Glue remaining two on each side below top stuffed bud. Continue gluing flowers, smallest to largest, on each side of the stem.

5. Glue leaves below flowers in same manner.

6. Insert pillow form inside cover.

Materials for Hollyhock

12" x 12" pillow form
12" x 12" black pillow cover
10" of 1 1/2" ombre white to purple wired ribbon
15" of 1" ombre green to pink wired ribbon
12" of 1 1/2" green wired ribbon
Black fabric pen
Scissors
Quick tack fabric glue
Tacky glue or hot glue gun and glue sticks

Directions

Follow directions for Foxglove, substituting ombre white to purple wired ribbon for ombre green to pink wired ribbon.

Materials for Hydrangea

12" x 12" pillow form
12" x 12" white pillow cover
2 yards of $^{1}/_{2}$" ombre green to blue wired ribbon
$^{1}/_{4}$ yard of $1^{1}/_{2}$" green wired ribbon
Scissors
Quick tack fabric glue
Tacky glue or hot glue gun and glue sticks

Directions

1. Cut the ombre wired ribbon into seventy-two 1" lengths. Make 18 flowers; see General Instructions for "Violets" on page 11.

2. Cut the green wired ribbon into three 3" lengths. Make a pointed leaf with one length; see General Instructions for "Pointed" leaves on page 16.

3. Slightly overlap remaining green ribbon lengths lengthwise. Glue lengths together along long wired edge. Fold and glue corners on one raw edge back, forming a point. Pinch and glue opposite end, forming a leaf.

4. Densely bunch flowers together and glue to center of pillow cover front.

5. Tuck leaves under flower bunch , one on each side, and glue to pillow cover front.

6. Insert pillow form inside cover.

THESE Cupids are forging
a ring of gold
To send with my love;
if I'm not too bold.

Elegant Pillows

Materials for Gold Basket

15" x 15" pillow form
15" x 15" green pillow cover
12" of 2" metallic-gold decorative trim
Metallic-gold floral hair
12" of $^3/_4$" metallic-gold decorative trim
13" of $^1/_4$" metallic-gold decorative trim
16" of $^5/_8$" violet wired ribbon
16" of $^5/_8$" dark violet wired ribbon
6" of $1^1/_2$" black wired ribbon
20" of $^5/_8$" ombre blue to white wired ribbon
$5^3/_4$" of $1^1/_2$" burgundy wired ribbon
6" of $2^5/_8$" plum wired ribbon
6" of $1^1/_2$" ombre rose to peach wired ribbon
3" of $1^1/_2$" ombre pink to green wired ribbon
6" of $1^1/_2$" ombre light blue to dark blue wired ribbon
4" of $1^1/_2$" gold grosgrain wired ribbon
3" of $^5/_8$" white wired ribbon
45" of 18-gauge stem wire
Red fabric paint
Paintbrush
Stuffing
Scissors
Quick tack fabric glue
Tacky glue or hot glue gun and glue sticks

Directions

1. Cut 2" metallic-gold decorative trim into two equal lengths. Glue edges together lengthwise, forming basket. Trim corners on one long edge, making a round base. Glue basket to pillow cover front 2" from bottom edge. Glue $^1/_4$" metallic-gold decorative trim around edges of basket, covering raw edges. Glue ends of $^3/_4$" metallic-gold decorative trim to top edge of basket, forming handle; see pattern on page 133. Glue a small amount of floral hair in the basket.

2. Cut a 12" length of $^5/_8$" violet wired ribbon. Tie ribbon into a bow. Fold and glue raw ends back, forming diagonal finished ends. Glue bow to top of handle.

3. Cut remaining $^5/_8$" violet wired ribbon and $^5/_8$" dark violet wired ribbon into twenty 1" lengths. Make five violets, attaching to stem wire; see General Instructions for "Violets" on page 11.

4. Paint red dots on black wired ribbon. When dry, cut into three 2" lengths. Make three berries; see General Instructions for "Berries" on page 18.

5. Cut $^5/_8$" ombre blue to white wired ribbon into ten 2" lengths. On one length, overlap and glue raw ends, forming a tube. Gather and glue one long edge, forming a flower cup. Repeat to make ten flower cups.

6. From burgundy wired ribbon, make a pansy, attaching to stem wire; see General Instructions for "Pansies" on page 10.

7. Overlap ends of $2^5/_8$" plum wired ribbon, forming a tube. Gather and glue one long edge, forming a cup. Fill with stuffing. Gather and glue remaining long edge, forming a plum.

8. Cut $1^1/_2$" ombre rose to peach wired ribbon into three 2" lengths. Repeat Step 7 for all lengths, making three peaches.

9. Cut $1^1/_2$" ombre pink to green wired ribbon into two equal lengths. Make a rosebud; see general Instructions for "Rosebuds" on page 14.

10. Cut 1 1/2" ombre light blue to dark blue wired ribbon into four 1 1/2" lengths. Make four pointed leaves; see General Instructions for "Pointed" leaves on page 16.

11. Cut 1 1/2" gold grosgrain wired ribbon into two equal lengths. On one length, overlap and glue raw ends, forming a tube. Gather and glue one long edge, forming a flower cup. Repeat to make two flower cups.

12. Cut 5/8" white wired ribbon into three 1" lengths. Make three lilies of the valley, attaching to stem wire; see General Instructions for "Lilies of the Valley" on page 15.

13. Glue flowers, fruit, and leaves to pillow cover front as desired or according to pattern on page 133.

GOLD BASKET PATTERN

Home Decor

Elegant Pillows

Materials for Rose Bowl

15" x 15" pillow form
15" x 15" green velvet pillow cover
¼ yard of decorative fabric
15" of 1½" gold wired ribbon
3" of 1" red wired ribbon
12" of ⅝" yellow wired ribbon
6" of 1½" brown wired ribbon
4" of 1½" orange wired ribbon
5¾" of 1½" burgundy wired ribbon
5¾" of 1½" purple wired ribbon
10½" of 1½" red wired ribbon
4" of 2" burgundy wired ribbon
¼ yard of 1½" ombre red to pink wired ribbon
7" of 1½" green wired ribbon
4" of 1½" cream wired ribbon
¼ yard of 1" purple wired ribbon
30" of 18-gauge stem wire
Black fabric paint
Paintbrush
Stuffing
Scissors
Quick tack fabric glue
Tacky glue or hot glue gun and glue sticks

Directions

1. Make bowl pattern on page 137. From decorative fabric, make a bowl. Fold and glue all raw edges under and glue to pillow cover front, 2" from bottom edge.

2. Cut the 1½" gold wired ribbon into eight 2" lengths. On one length, overlap and glue raw ends, forming a tube. Gather and glue one long edge, forming a cup. Repeat to make eight tubes. Fill three gathered tubes with stuffing. Gather and glue remaining long edge, forming three stuffed buds. To form foxglove, glue tubes and buds to pillow cover front according to pattern on page 137.

3. Paint black dots on 1" red wired ribbon. When dry, cut into three 3" lengths. Make three berries; see General Instructions for "Berries" on page 18.

4. Cut ⅝" yellow wired ribbon into eight 1½" lengths. Cut a 1" length from brown wired ribbon. Make an eight-petaled daisy, attaching to stem wire; see General Instructions for "Daisies" on page 12.

5. Cut 1½" orange wired ribbon into two equal lengths. On one length, overlap and glue raw ends, forming a tube. Gather and glue one long edge, forming a cup. Fill with stuffing. Gather and glue remaining long edge, forming acorn. Repeat with remaining length. Cut 1½" brown wired ribbon into two equal lengths. Fold one long edge forward and wrap around one acorn; glue. Pinch and glue ends. Repeat on other acorn.

6. From 1½" burgundy and purple wired ribbons, make two pansies, attaching to stem wire; see General Instructions for "Pansies" on page 10.

7. Cut 1½" red wired ribbon into seven 1½" lengths. Make one rosebud and one mature rosebud; see general Instructions for "Rosebuds" on page 14.

8. Cut the 2" burgundy wired ribbon into two equal lengths. On one length, overlap and glue raw ends, forming a tube. Gather and glue one long edge, forming a cup. Fill with stuffing. Gather and glue remaining long edge, forming a plum. Repeat to make two plums.

9. Cut $1^{1}/_{2}$" ombre red to pink wired ribbon into two 3" lengths. Glue red edges together lengthwise, forming a wide length. Overlap and glue raw ends, forming a tube. Gather and glue one long edge, forming a cup. Fill with stuffing. Gather and glue remaining long edge, forming an apple.

10. Cut $1^{1}/_{2}$" green wired ribbon and remaining $1^{1}/_{2}$" ombre red to pink wired ribbon into $1^{1}/_{2}$" lengths. Make four green and two pink pointed leaves; see General Instructions for "Pointed" leaves on page 16. From remaining length of green wired ribbon, make a leaf cap, attaching to rosebud; see General Instructions for "Leaf Caps" on page 18.

11. Cut $1^{1}/_{2}$" cream wired ribbon into two equal lengths. On one length, overlap and glue raw ends, forming a tube. Gather and glue one long edge, forming a flower cup. Repeat with remaining length.

12. Cut 1" purple wired ribbon into nine 1" lengths. Place a pea-sized ball of stuffing in center of one length. Cover ball with ribbon, forming a grape. Wrap and secure ribbon with thread. Cut away excess ribbon, being careful not to cut through thread. Repeat to make nine grapes.

13. Glue flowers, fruit and leaves to pillow cover front as desired or according to pattern on page 137.

ROSE BOWL PATTERN

Home Decor

Elegant Pillows

Materials for Nosegay

15" x 15" pillow form
15" x 15" black pillow cover
$^1/_4$ yard of 2" metallic-gold decorative trim
Metallic-gold floral hair
One 2" metallic-gold tassel
16$^1/_2$" of 1$^1/_2$" ombre rose to peach wired ribbon
12" of $^5/_8$" white wired ribbon
1" of 1$^1/_2$" brown wired ribbon
5$^3/_4$" of 1$^1/_2$" peach wired ribbon
5$^3/_4$" of 1$^1/_2$" purple wired ribbon
12" of $^1/_2$" white wired ribbon
6$^1/_2$" of 1$^1/_2$" green wired ribbon
30" of 18-gauge stem wire
Black fabric pen
Stuffing
Scissors
Quick tack fabric glue
Tacky glue or hot glue gun and glue sticks

Directions

1. Cut 2" metallic-gold decorative trim into two equal lengths. Glue lengths together lengthwise, forming a wider length. Overlap and glue raw ends, forming a cone. Glue cone, narrow end down, to pillow cover front, 2" from bottom edge. Glue tassel to bottom of cone. Stuff cone with floral hair.

2. Cut 1$^1/_2$" ombre rose to cream wired ribbon into nine 1$^1/_2$" lengths. Make two rosebuds and one mature rosebud, attaching to stem wire; see general Instructions for "Rosebuds" on page 14.

3. Cut $^5/_8$" yellow wired ribbon into eight 1$^1/_2$" lengths. Make an eight-petaled daisy, attaching to stem wire; see General Instructions for "Daisies" on page 12.

4. From peach and purple 1$^1/_2$" wired ribbons, make two pansies, attaching to stem wire; see General Instructions for "Pansies" on page 10.

5. Cut $^1/_2$" white wired ribbon into eleven 1" lengths. Make two violets and one violet bud, attaching to stem wire; see General Instructions for "Violets" on page 11.

6. Overlap and glue raw ends of remaining $^1/_2$" white wired ribbon length. Gather and glue one long edge, forming a flower cup.

7. Cut 1$^1/_2$" green wired ribbon into three 1$^1/_2$" lengths. Make three pointed leaves, attaching to stem wire; see General Instructions for "Pointed" leaves on page 16.

8. Cut remaining length of green wired ribbon into two equal lengths. Make two leaf caps, attaching one to each rosebud; see General Instructions for "Leaf Caps" on page 18.

9. Glue flowers and leaves to pillow cover front as desired or according to pattern on page 140.

10. Insert pillow form inside cover.

NOSEGAY PATTERN

Metric Equivalence Chart

MM-Millimetres CM-Centimetres

INCHES TO MILLIMETRES AND CENTIMETRES

INCHES	MM	CM	INCHES	CM	INCHES	CM
1/8	3	0.9	9	22.9	30	76.2
1/4	6	0.6	10	25.4	31	78.7
3/8	10	1.0	11	27.9	32	81.3
1/2	13	1.3	12	30.5	33	83.8
5/8	16	1.6	13	33.0	34	86.4
3/4	19	1.9	14	35.6	35	88.9
7/8	22	2.2	15	38.1	36	91.4
1	25	2.5	16	40.6	37	94.0
1 1/4	32	3.2	17	43.2	38	96.5
1 1/2	38	3.8	18	45.7	39	99.1
1 3/4	44	4.4	19	48.3	40	101.6
2	51	5.1	20	50.8	41	104.1
2 1/2	64	6.4	21	53.3	42	106.7
3	76	7.6	22	55.9	43	109.2
3 1/2	89	8.9	23	58.4	44	111.8
4	102	10.2	24	61.0	45	114.3
4 1/2	114	11.4	25	63.5	46	116.8
5	127	12.7	26	66.0	47	119.4
6	152	15.2	27	68.6	48	121.9
7	178	17.8	28	71.1	49	124.5
8	203	20.3	29	73.7	50	127.0

YARDS TO METRES

YARDS	METRES	YARDS	METRES	YARDS	METRES	YARDS	METRES	YARDS	METRES
1/8	0.11	2 1/8	1.94	4 1/8	3.77	6 1/8	5.60	8 1/8	7.43
1/4	0.23	2 1/4	2.06	4 1/4	3.89	6 1/4	5.72	8 1/4	7.54
3/8	0.34	2 3/8	2.17	4 3/8	4.00	6 3/8	5.83	8 3/8	7.66
1/2	0.46	2 1/2	2.29	4 1/2	4.11	6 1/2	5.94	8 1/2	7.77
5/8	0.57	2 5/8	2.40	4 5/8	4.23	6 5/8	6.06	8 5/8	7.89
3/4	0.69	2 3/4	2.51	4 3/4	4.34	6 3/4	6.17	8 3/4	8.00
7/8	0.80	2 7/8	2.63	4 7/8	4.46	6 7/8	6.29	8 7/8	8.12
1	0.91	3	2.74	5	4.57	7	6.40	9	8.23
1 1/8	1.03	3 1/8	2.86	5 1/8	4.69	7 1/8	6.52	9 1/8	8.34
1 1/4	1.14	3 1/4	2.97	5 1/4	4.80	7 1/4	6.63	9 1/4	8.46
1 3/8	1.26	3 3/8	3.09	5 3/8	4.91	7 3/8	6.74	9 3/8	8.57
1 1/2	1.37	3 1/2	3.20	5 1/2	5.03	7 1/2	6.86	9 1/2	8.69
1 5/8	1.49	3 5/8	3.31	5 5/8	5.14	7 5/8	6.97	9 5/8	8.80
1 3/4	1.60	3 3/4	3.43	5 3/4	5.26	7 3/4	7.09	9 3/4	8.92
1 7/8	1.71	3 7/8	3.54	5 7/8	5.37	7 7/8	7.20	9 7/8	9.03
2	1.83	4	3.66	6	5.49	8	7.32	10	9.14

Index